2/21/0

MW01180945

To Mary —
A dear friend and fellow
traveler — with all my best!

Are you a Dreamer?

Cordially,
Dr. Kim Dresour

Rediscovering The American Dream

The American Dream Party of the United States of America

by

Dr. Tim Dosemagen

Bloomington, IN Milton Keynes, UK

AuthorHouse™
1663 Liberty Drive,
Suite 200
Bloomington, IN 47403
www.authorhouse.com
Phone: 1-800-839-8640

AuthorHouse™ UK Ltd.
500 Avebury Boulevard
Central Milton Keynes, MK9 2BE
www.authorhouse.co.uk
Phone: 08001974150

First published by AuthorHouse
ISBN: 978-1-4259-8111-2 (sc)   1/11/2007

Library of Congress Control Number: 2006910769

Printed in the United States of America
Bloomington, Indiana

This book is printed on acid-free paper.

Previous Works by Dr. Dosemagen:

Prodigies – A Warring Species and the Human Heart

The Impossible

The Trigger

Dedication

This book is dedicated to the heightened awareness of the American people, who must possess a clear-headed recognition of the failures of this world, in order to avoid mis-reaching at home and abroad, which always leads to failure.

We can learn much from the world's failures.

To **Senator Joe McCarthy** = That Oddball Oz Bellowing Behind Cheese Curtains. He took on ghosts at a time when being anti-Communist meant gaining votes from the party faithful, and mis-reached when his puffery and zeal outran the decency of his Senatorial chamber mates. A true failure.

To **Vice President Al Gore** = That Great Gaseous Bloviating Bio-Blimp. A fortunate son of Tennessee political power, he was uniquely able to wrestle defeat out of the hands of a 543,816 vote victory in the Presidential elections of 2000, at the hands of an inarticulate, bumbling Texas transplant. A true double failure, he not only lost his home state of Tennessee's vital electoral votes, but also lost the ultimate decision amongst the black-robed Supreme Court, 5-4.

To **Venezuelan President Hugo Chavez** = That Petroleum-based Bombastic Banana Republican. He came to New York and found the devil, only it turned out that El Diablo was closer than the U.N. pulpit, waiting in the hotel room mirror. A true loser, he imitated and idolized dying dictators, fighting like a Rebel for Leftist causes beyond his little nation's oily scope. Maracaibo's buried treasures are the most this pompous pirate will ever steal.

To **Osama Bin Laden** = That Wealthy Wayfarer Beckoning Apocalyptic Appeal Amongst Poisoned Minds, Suicidal Quitters and Jilted Jihadis. A true loser, he tried to stop the march of modernization amongst his brethren, ignoring the fact that history does not reward terror, and progress does not cotton to those who will deny one half of humanity its right to excel. Terror Boy - your life as a cave dweller becomes your deeds as a coward, shyly exposing yourself only to video cameras. Your days here are numbered; a swine-ridden eternity is closing in.

And to **President George W. Bush** = An at best average performing, stammering child of privilege, who finally and eloquently proved to the American polity that, like the Romans 2,000 years antecedent, when the best a Republic of 300 million people can do in 12 years is to elect the son of a former President to the highest office in the land, the vision that was Democracy in Philadelphia back in 1776 is in drastic need of rediscovery and rejuvenation. Known forevermore to historians as President Debt, W's legacy was more added national debt than any other President, while sowing and riding incessant fear, and demanding no fiscal sacrifice from the people. "Keep spending," he told us. Thanks for showing your fellow Americans the errors of their ways, George – mission accomplished.

Contents

I - Prologue

The American Dream Party of the *United States of America* is all about moving forward the very best ideas of the generations of Americans now coming of age, namely, **Generation X** (those born between 1964 and 1975), **Generation Y** (those born between 1976 and 1989), and **The Millennials** (those born between 1990 and 2005).

American Dreamers acknowledge that our great nation has been placed in serious risk of losing its position of global leadership; as we witness the decline of our great Republic, stunned, we are motivated to act upon it, refusing to accept a national mediocrity.

We have sadly inherited a nation with over $8.4 trillion in National Debt, currently adding to this debt by borrowing $8 thousand per second, in good economic times. *American Dreamers* pledge to eliminate this debt, stopping this borrowing, largely from the East-Asians.

We have mis-launched the Global War On Terror without a stated focus, absent benchmarked objectives, adrift without a targeted completion date, occupying countries with 19th Century tactics in an age of 21st Century asymmetric warfare, alienating former allies with a 'go it alone' diplomatic strategy, funding this effort absent a unifying national sacrifice, borrowing money from our children to referee a sectarian civil war between peoples who despise us, adding to our National Debt. *American Dreamers* pledge to end this useless involvement in Iraq, properly refocusing our efforts on the quarantine and elimination of the cancer - Radical Islam.

We have slouched from the manned exploration of space, having last landed a person on a body other than the earth well over three decades ago. *American Dreamers* pledge to reassert our birthrights as a space-faring nation, reaching for the manned exploration of Mars, and beyond...while accelerating the necessary search for extraterrestrial intelligence.

We have stagnated in the development of a greater American community, fractionalizing our citizenry along ethnicities and languages. *American Dreamers* pledge to forge better intergenerational relationships, while inculcating a sense of what it means to be an American, the glory of national purpose, and the beauty that is Americanism.

We have so degenerated the vision that was Democracy back in Philadelphia in 1776, that Americans now find themselves the inheritors of an indistinguishable two-party system, primarily run by wealthy practitioners from the narrow fields of Law, who administer an unresponsive, bloated plutocracy, where the closest Federal representation available to any American is one Representative for every 700,000 citizens. *Ameri-*

can Dreamers pledge to use modern technologies to empower each and every American to vote directly on the Federal level, wresting power from the hands of the Republicrats.

Will Rogers is attributed as having come up with the following: "I ain't no Democrat - Democrats love other people so much, they'll give 'em your money. I ain't no Republican, either - Republicans was born on second base and think they hit a double!"

Now that's straight shootin'!

Fellow Americans, this is your wake up call. Are you ready to move forward?

We now make the case for good government starting at the <u>very</u> top. The very moment a nation begins to expect less from its leaders, the culture begins to decline, and ultimately fall. Look at the total difference, in just the 33 years between Eisenhower and Clinton.

Ancient Chinese saying go: **"When the king is rotten, the kingdom rots."**

How will we reset the impeccable standards and highest demands for our top leadership? For surely, if we are to survive and grow, America must re-establish high standards.

How can we improve upon this constitutional republic, to break from the "lesser of two evils" quadrennial choice making into which the presidential selection process has evolved, or, worse yet, the biennial Congressional reelection of incumbents?

The elections of 2016 are coming – are we ready to take back America?

Join us - *Become a Dreamer!*

Visit http://theamericandreamparty.org

- Share ideas with fellow Dreamers now. Email your views and comments.

- Send your money to the Republicrats. We want your dreams.

- Become a member ~ Your American Dream Party official membership certificate is ready to be downloaded.

- Welcome aboard!

II - War on the National Debt of the United States

In 1979, President James Earl Carter expressed alarm at the massive size of the burgeoning National Debt, which then stood on the brink of an astounding $1 trillion dollars. Today, our National Debt now exceeds $8.4 trillion dollars.

We have become the laughing stock of the world. Globally, "American" is now synonymous with living beyond one's means, being super-sized, living for to-day, flashing bling, living large, borrowing excessively to drive a Caddy while renting an apartment.

What's worse? Today, even during "good" economic times (5 -6% unemployment), we have borrowed near-ly $1 billion per day, or $10,000 per second, posting a $350 billion deficit in just 2005, alone. Under current projections, in our lifetimes, these United States will do what even Imperial Rome, in all of its grotesque excesses, never accomplished – the size of our Na-tional Debt will eclipse the size of our gross national product.

Who's to blame? Let's be frank – Tom Brokaw's "Greatest Generation," the generation that survived the Great Depression and went off to defeat Nazi Germany and Imperial Japan, came home after The Big One and threw themselves one whale of a party. They called their retirement plan Social Security. They called their retirement medical plan *Medicare.* They called their college education *The G.I. Bill.* They called their attempt to rectify centuries of racial injustice through a lazy, feel good war on poverty *The Great Society.* They spent trillions, and it worked well for them, whether they had a D next to their names or an R.

Who's going to pick up the tab? The Late-Boomers, Generation Xers, Generation Yers, and Millennials, whom the Greatest Generation had the bald temerity to label as the "Me Generation".

In one of history's most ironic twists, after enjoying a unparalleled prosperity, the real "Me Generation," those who were the most selfish, who thirsted for instant gratification, and wanted it all right now, are now leaving us – deep in debt, and in serious risk of losing our economic independence.

As for the society, actually, one can't really blame folks for being about "ME" - Americans have been trained in selfishness by a generation of Americans whose leadership has, since 1980, brought the nation's national debt all the way from just under one trillion dollars to well over eight trillion dollars. In but one generation, we have nearly filled our cup to its double, with the size of our national debt ($8.4 trillion) nearing the size of our entire economy ($12 trillion).

We are now only one hard recession away from this eventuality.

Brokaw's "Greatest Generation", whether it had a "D" or an "R" next to it, survived the Depression stoically, won the Good War valiantly, and then it came home, throwing itself one whale of a party, well beyond any excesses in recorded history. It all started in the 1980's under two great "ME" leaders - Ronald Reagan and Tip O'Neill. "ME" loved them both, and why not?

Pity the poor Romans, making coins out of metal... it took three men - one to strike the obverse, one to flip the slug carefully from one die to the next, with a special tong, and then one more man to strike the reverse. In the days of their greatest excesses, the Roman Emperors had over 20 mints running at full throttle, in places like Gaul, some producing over a million Cistercians per day, the coins valued on a combination of the base metal, and the good name of the Emperor whose face appeared on the obverse.

At the end of the 20th Century and well into the 21st, the "ME" Americans just issued treasury bonds - borrowing from their progeny with an unprecedented profligacy.

They funded their educations with the G.I. Bill. That was about "ME". They funded their retirements with Social Security. That was about "ME". They funded their retirement healthcare with Medicare, throwing in prescription drug benefits. That was about "ME".

Remember the idea of a "lock box" for the protection of Social Security surpluses, floated by Democratic Presidential candidate Al Gore back in 2000? "ME" voted, and the answer has left the Social Security trust fund with nothing in it but I.O.U.s, allowing ever more borrowing, while the Republicratic Congress shifts budgetary line items in an ongoing fiscal horror show of the most shameful chicanery.

Picking up this tab? Late Baby Boomers, Gen-X, Gen-Y, and The Millennials.

American Dreamers recognize that this is unethical behavior on an unparalleled scale. How could American businesses have ignored it? How could American families have ignored it?

Bankruptcy? There's no shame in it anymore - Americans did over a million in just one year - 2005 - and in "good" economic times. Sure beats picking up the tab owed to those nasty creditors, right?

Personal debt? The average American holds over $7,000 in revolving debt, not to mention borrowing for automobiles, and financing home purchases. We have learned well from "ME", haven't we?

The generations that follow, in picking up that 8.4 trillion dollar tab (and growing), will well remember the "Greatest "ME" Generation". They fought, they voted, they won, and they spent their country's future into great economic peril. We live in an Age of Debt - national, corporate, personal, and generational.

And it is accelerating. Think about it this way. In "good" economic times, with 5-6% unemployment, America is borrowing $200 to $400 billion dollars for "ME" each and every year. These monies are increasingly coming from around the globe - specifically, East Asia, where over 15% of our national debt is now owned by the Koreans, the Japanese and the Chinese.

Who increasingly owns the American national destiny?

Interestingly, if you lined up eight trillion dollar bills, at six inches per bill, end-to-end from the surface of the earth and into outer space, with $12,000 equaling one mile's distance, which planet's orbit do you think "ME's" debt would exceed - Mars, Jupiter, or Saturn? Good money says the answer is Saturn.

While the age of debt defines and actually served Brokaw's "Greatest Generation," it is entirely unacceptable to American Dreamers.

In notes on Deontology by Charles D. Kay, it is written that: "Kant's theory is an example of a **deontological or duty-based ethics**: it judges morality by examining the nature of actions and the will of agents rather than goals achieved. (Roughly, a deontological theory looks at inputs rather than outcomes.) One reason for the shift away from consequences to duties is that, in spite of our best efforts, we cannot control the future. We are praised or blamed for actions within our control, and that includes our willing, not our achieving. This is not to say that Kant did not care about the outcomes of our actions--we all wish for good things. Rather Kant insisted that as far as the moral evaluation of our actions was concerned, consequences did not matter."

Those who made America a nation of profligate and as yet unrepentant borrowers, like Kant, said "consequences be damned." They saw the need to borrow (to stimulate the economy, to keep the retired comfortable, to pay the retirees' medical bills, to buy the retirees' medicine, etc. etc. etc.) and borrowed without a care for the consequences that their children and grandchildren will most certainly realize.

Americans now face a dark future of hyper-inflation, a shattered dollar, Social Security at 75 (and worth very little), no Medicare of any value, and a completely ruined economy, well within our lifetimes.

Dreamers recognize that absent a sound national fiscal policy, eliminating structural deficits, there will be no way to eliminate our national debt, except to make a dollar worth a dime, and a dime worth a penny. That's called hyperinflation, and it heralds the downfall of the world's longest experiment in government of the people, by the people, and for the people.

Alas, the filthy byproduct of a convenient deontology practiced by "ME" in the America we know and love. Enough!

Kay goes on: "Deontological ethics is strongest in many of the areas where utilitarianism is weakest. In an ethics of duty, the ends can never justify the means. Individual **human rights** are acknowledged and inviolable. We need not consider the satisfaction of harmful desires in our moral deliberations. In practice, however, Kant's ethics poses two great problems that lead many to reject it:

> 1. Unlike the proportionality that comes out of the utility principle, the categorical imperative yields *only absolutes*. Actions either pass or fail with no allowance for a "gray area." Moreover, the rigid lines are often drawn in unlikely places. For example, lying is always wrong-- even the "polite lie."
>
> 2. *Moral dilemmas* are created when duties come in conflict, and there is no mechanism for solving them. Utilitarianism permits a ready comparison of all actions, and if a set of alternatives have the same expected utility, they are equally good. Conflicting duties, however, may require that I perform logically or physically incompatible actions, and my failure to do any one is itself a moral wrong."

The American Dream Party's answer to our gargantuan National Debt problem is two-fold:

1.) Balanced budgets, eliminating the need to borrow money from the East-Asians.

2.) War on the National Debt of the United States.

The first action will remove the purse strings from the drunken Republicrats. The second action will be resolved through the blood, sweat and tears of the recipients of the "Greatest Generation's" legacy. We'll clean up after their party, because as patriotic Americans, we know that it must be done if we are to survive as a nation, absent hyper-inflation and a dollar crash.

From aluminum can collections to the sales of War Bonds, through the War On Debt, we'll get the job done. Our parents and grandparents leave us no choice.

III - Border Security

On September 11th, 2001, 19 religious zealots on 4 airplanes suddenly and ruthlessly attacked New York and Washington, in a two-hour operation, catching the nation completely by surprise, killing 3,000 citizens.

These attacks, when accounting for their clean-up, subsequent rebuilding, their dampening effects on the economy, our subsequent invasions of Afghanistan and Iraq, the establishment of the TSA, the establishment of the DHS, the bailout of the airline industry, the wars in Iraq and Afghanistan, and now the run-up to war with Iran, cost the United States a 4% dent in an $12 trillion economy.

We were asleep. History will forgive the American citizenry who woke up on 9/11/01. It must never be allowed to happen again, and to keep it from recurring, our borders with Canada and Mexico, as well as our seaboards, must be completely and vigilantly sealed.

Let Americans well remember that on September 11th, 2001, we had the best global defense structure that $400 billion could buy. It failed to stop 19 men on four airplanes in a two hour operation.

A mansion on a hill, no matter how grand, will fall victim to termites if left unprotected. Our borders remain naked. Our new National Defense Structure must refocus on pest control, if we are to remain a free people enjoying a vibrant economy.

IV - National Defense

The American Dream Party supports a robust and capable military, fully prepared to meet the challenges of the 21st Century in all respects, with efficiency of operations.

America's defense posture and relationships must be based upon preservation over profit. The first mission of the government is to protect its citizenry.

Governing bodies that place citizens at risk while pursuing profits are wholly corrupt and un-American.

America must be willing to act alone, if necessary. National defense is not about winning popularity contests – it is all about protecting the citizenry.

America must be willing to use surprise. Surprise is the antithesis of sluggish, plodding, public coalition building, signaling intentions to the enemy.

America must refuse to target civilians. However, the citizens of state supporters of terror, as tacit and implicit support of terrorists, relinquish their neutrality, joining the cause of enemy combatants.

America must maintain in a state of constant offensive readiness, with an emphasis on discriminatory tactical operations, and progressive warfare.

The American Dream Party envisions an America that is dually protected by a *Global Defense Force* and a *National Defense Force*, operating in tandem.

The Global Defense Force will unify fighting units and strategies, resulting in efficiencies of weapons procurement and development, combined offensive operations, and combined Special Operations Forces. The armed services of the Defense Department (Army, Navy, Air Force and Marine Corps) will be united into one uniformed service. As we sharpen our spears for the 21st Century and beyond, it will be the united Special Operations Forces that will yield the greatest strategic improvements to our Global Defense Force.

We support a defense structure comprised of 8 aircraft carrier battle groups, 30 SLBM platforms, 100 fast attack subs, 10 aerial combat wings, 10 tactical fighter wings, 3 heavy armored divisions, 12 light divisions, fast attack / shock / marine forces of 200,000 active duty personnel, and a unified Special Operations Force of 150,000 active duty personnel. Total active duty armed forces will not exceed 2,000,000 personnel in times of peace, and total peacetime defense spending shall be capped at 15% of the Federal Budget.

The Pentagon may elect to sell weapons to allied nations as a source of additional funding. We recognize that World War II ended over 60 years ago, and the Cold War ended over 15 years ago, therefore, we advocate for a complete withdrawal of American ground combat elements from the European Continent, and anticipate withdrawal of all American ground combat forces from the Korean Peninsula following Korean reunification.

The Coast Guard, augmenting the good works being undertaken by our nascent Department of Homeland Security, will be joined by volunteer citizens in the newly created National Defense Force.

Through the NDF, American citizens must be enlisted in the necessary task of identifying, tracking, and reporting on the spread of the cancer that is Radical Islam, here within our borders.

Through the NDF, American citizens must be enlisted in the vital and unending struggle to establish and maintain drum-tight borders, stopping the invasion of illegal and unwelcome border trespassers.

Through the NDF, American citizens must be enlisted in the war being fought on the streets of our great nation, reporting on illegal drug transport, sales, and use.

V - Replacing The House of Representatives With The People

When the founders of the American Republic created The Congress, they envisioned a federal legislative body that would forever maintain the closest contact with The People. The idea was brilliant, the concept simple: a bicameral legislative body, including a House of Representatives comprised of average citizens and subject to frequent change, alongside a more august Senate, comprised of leading intellectuals, more stable, and less subject to the whims of the masses. Alongside an Executive and a Judicial branch, The Congress would most effectively represent the direct will of the people; indeed, once upon a time, it did.

Today, over 300,000,000 Americans are represented by 435 Congressmen. The closest that the will of any one citizen will be felt at the Federal level is reflected in the ratio of Congressional representation, now standing at 1:690,000. At the time of our founding, in an age of horse drawn carriages, lamp signals and hand written letters, it made sense to design such a representative system. After all, to be effective, big government had to be administered by a minimum of its citizenry, and Democracy didn't have a prayer of efficiency if all citizens couldn't walk or ride to the frequently held face-to-face meetings. The system worked, and using the technology at hand, served us well for over 200 years.

Today, The Congress of the United States has grown into a hulking, expensive, unresponsive and corrupt monstrosity. A simple calculation of the base salaries of each Representative, along with their benefits, along with their personal operating expenses, along with the total costs of their staffs, along with the costs of their committees, travel, office space, materials, franking privileges, meals, pensions, etc., comes to over $2,000,000 per Congressional district, or about a billion dollars for all 435 districts.

In addition, there are 66 lobbyists for each Congressman. These power brokers use any means of persuasion at their disposal, making Congressmen and their family members rich, and The System rewards their efforts with a steady stream of endless pork, typified by the $200,000,000 "Bridge to Nowhere" project in Alaska, linking the Alaskan mainland to a sparsely populated island. Today's Congressmen never stop fundraising, and they work less and less for We The People, and more for their own enrichment.

Recently, our Do-Nothing 109th Congress, while commanding six figure salaries, worked less than 45 full legislative days out of an entire year.

The payoff for all this governmental overhead? You, I, and every American have but one voice for every Milwaukee, Wisconsin-sized chunk of the populace, nationwide. The people we see in Washington, our "representatives" are behaving poorly.

How low has democracy slouched? Consider this excerpt from Jonathan Turley, which ran in The Forum of USA Today, circa 2006:

"In its waning months, the 109th Congress has finally achieved a status in politics that the 1919 Black Sox achieved in sports: It is a symbol of utter corruption. Over the past two years, the congressional scandals have traversed the universe from the gross to the grandiose to the grotesque: visits from call girls, gifts of Rolls Royces and fancy commodes, sweetheart deals for contractors, high-paying lobbyist jobs for under-achieving children, free vacations for members and their families."

Remember, fellow Americans – these scoundrels are supposed to be working for we, the people. This is what happened to the vision that great minds conceived in Philadelphia. Welcome to Rome. Turley continues:

"Yet, if the young boy saying 'say it ain't so' to Shoeless Joe Jackson perfectly summed up the betrayal of the 1919 World Series, the young male pages pursued by former GOP congressman Mark Foley of Florida perfectly summed up the betrayal of the 109th Congress. The public clearly suspects that, in dealing with Foley, House leaders were more concerned with protecting a House seat than a House page. In a CNN poll, 75% of

Americans say the Republicans failed to act responsibly, and 52% believe a coverup was attempted.

"If the page scandal captures the raw depravity that is the 109th Congress, the proposed solution captures its raw audacity. Faced with the abuse of children, some lawmakers have called for the removal of the children. First voiced by Rep. Ray LaHood, R-Ill., some members have indicated that they would terminate the page service after almost 200 years of tradition. As LaHood explained, "We should not subject young men and women to this kind of activity, this kind of vulnerability." When asked whether he was suggesting that his colleagues cannot be trusted with children, he responded, "Well, that's pretty obvious."

"Though this might seem like preventing bank robbery by getting rid of trains, it makes sense in the parallel moral universe of the 109th Congress. Indeed, these lawmakers appear to have adopted Oscar Wilde's rule that the only way to be rid of temptation is to yield to it.

"Hence, the LaHood proposal: If one cannot deliver one's colleagues from temptation, you must remove the temptation from one's colleagues. Presumably, only then could pedophilic members be able to fully focus on the public good.

"Under this logic, pages are the problem – lurking in the halls like sirens of destruction for lawmakers. Apostle Peter warned of such temptation from the devil "as a roaring lion walketh about, seeking whom he may devour." Only the fearful would survive, he cautioned, and "your bretheren" would be brought low by "the same afflictions."

"Fortunately, LaHood's solution has little support. Yet he and his colleagues may be on to something. While they accept that some members cannot be relied upon to exercise self-restraint with children, they do not address other temptations that have brought their bretheren low. For example, why not bar lobbyists? If lawmakers have difficulty showing restraint around children, they've shown even less restraint around lobbyists.

"The scandals are too numerous to detail, but various members are under criminal investigation, indictment, or federal custody.

"Former majority leader Tom DeLay is under indictment in Texas; Rep. William Jefferson, D-La., is still trying to explain $90,000 wrapped in foil in his freezer; GOP congressman Bob Ney of Ohio will likely face prison time after pleading guilty to conspiracy and making false statements while former colleague Randy "Duke" Cunningham of California is already in prison for taking more than $2.4 million in bribes.

"In addition to various lawmakers still under investigation in the scandal involving lobbyist Jack Abramoff, members such as Speaker Dennis Hastert, R-Ill., Rep. Alan Mollohan, D-W.Va., and others have been accused of self-dealing in steering hundreds of millions of federal funds for personal benefit.

"Dozens of lawmakers have been criticized for having children or spouses working for lobbyists or accepting exorbitant vacations from outside groups. Just this week, the FBI searched homes in an investigation of whether Rep. Curt Weldon, R-Pa., used his position to steer lobbying jobs to his daughter.

"LaHood himself has been accused of questionable deals with lobbyists, including his earmarking of millions of dollars to benefit projects and firms. Some of these earmarks involved lobbyists who once sat on La-Hood's fundraising committee. (After the Abramoff scandal, LaHood suddenly announced that he would get rid of his lobbyist-laden committee.) Likewise, La-Hood and his wife have also been criticized for their free trips abroad, including one to China paid by the not-for-profit Aspen Institute.

"Applying LaHood's logic, the solution is simple: no lobbyists, no lobbying scandals. Indeed, it is possible to remove every historic temptation from the halls of Congress so members can walk to the floor without a distracting thought. We could ban call girls (common in past scandals) and even order both genders to cover themselves with burqas while visiting congressional offices. The result would be a hermetically sealed, temptation-free environment for our morally challenged leaders.

"Yet, it is sometimes more efficient to fence in a risk rather than to force everyone to fence it out. It follows that it would be far better to fence in our lawmakers rather than fence out temptations such as children, pets or suggestively arranged plants.

"Neither efficiency nor morality, however, have been particularly great influences on the 109th Congress. And it is a measure of how out of touch LaHood and company have become that they would address the lack of restraint of some lawmakers by eliminating all pages.

"I am no biblical scholar, but when Peter promised that "the Lord knoweth how to deliver the godly out of temptations," I don't think this is what he had in mind, adds Turley.

If you are feeling a little let down, join the over 50% of your fellow citizens who don't even vote in Congressional elections, completely opting out of national policy making.

It has gotten this bad, the Founders are furious, and must be kicking in their coffins.

Not to mention the fact that, for all our hard earned tax dollars, the people's money, we get servants of the people with time on their hands to send suggestive emails to pages, who hide thousands of ill-gotten dollars in their freezers, who use postage to convert into personal spending cash, with high crimes and misdemeanors far worse left unmentioned here. The entire body has become corrupt, lazy, and even worse for the people, unresponsive.

Are Dreamers unfair in accusing the House of Representatives for being unresponsive? To find out, join us, if you will, in an experiment in early 21st Century Democracy. Forget the phone, the fax, or the letter – settle for nothing less than the speed of light.

Go to www.house.gov, look up your Congressman, and write them an email, with a question that concerns you. Please be careful to add a question to the email, or the experiment in Democracy will not work. For example:

"Dear Congressman: Hi. I'm really concerned about the quality of the state parks in our district. What are you doing, and what can I do, to help keep our state parks free of graffiti, trash and vagrants? By the way, how's the weather in Washington? With best wishes, and kindest regards, your citizen, (insert name and email address here)."

{For even more fun, send this chapter, along with your personal story of the effects of technology & downsizing on your career, asking for your Congressman's personal take.}

Send the email, and mark your clock, keeping in mind that this is an important experiment. If it helps, pretend Benjamin Franklin is sitting by your side, and give Ol' Ben a wink, as you click "send." As you wait for your response from the $1,000,000,000.00 House of one branch of the government of our representative Democracy, the very branch designed to be your direct federal voice, we'll make you a bet: Over 50% of you won't even get a response. Dead air – cyber limbo – ice. Go ahead - Try it!

Dreamers wish it weren't so, but we've tried it ourselves. Some of you, a select few, will receive an automatically generated email response acknowledging your message, and that will be the end of it. Fewer yet, perhaps one out of 1,000 of you, will receive an automatically generated form letter explaining your Congressman's position on the broad area of your topic.

A chosen few of you, perhaps several dozen citizens (depending whether or not your name matches your Congressman's database of sustaining, meaningful donors, or persons of high profile or great community influence) will receive a personal response penned by a Congressional staffer, rubber stamped with your Congressman's signature block. And finally, one of you may receive a follow-up telephone call, asking for details on your email.

No one will be invited to discuss the matter personally with your Congressman. And, to be sure, no one will be invited to fly to Washington to meet with your Congressman, face-to-face. Lastly, not a soul will be invited to discuss the matter in a home or business visit by your Congressman. (Too expensive and time consuming – we get it!) Sadly, that's the state of affairs in today's America, here in the world's best and brightest shining beacon of representative Democracy. This will not stand, because American Dreamers know that the vision that was Democracy in Philadelphia awaits our rediscovery.

What's even more amazing is that we annually shell out over a billion dollars for this travesty of under-representation, and astoundingly, most people don't mind. The system is so broken, people will beef about slow services, potholes, influence peddling and broken campaign promises sooner than they'll demand action from their invisible Congressmen. It's gotten so bad, that each two years, over 90% of the time, sitting Congressmen are simply re-elected by an apathetic public who make a greater statement by not casting any vote at all, voting with their feet by staying away from the polls.

Is this what the brilliant minds of great men conceived in Philadelphia 230 years ago? Rest assured, this current state of affairs will not last, as history has shown. It is going to change in one of two ways.

Either through apathy or disenfranchisement, the people will eventually lose their federal voice entirely (e.g. The Roman Empire cum Republic), or We The People will take back what we were given by the founders.

Indeed, we must continually improve upon our Democracy if our Republic is to survive. It's what Ben, Alexander, Thomas, John, Samuel and George would want!

The American Dream Party proposal:

Eliminate The House of Representatives from The Congress of the United States, replacing it with The People. Please weigh the positives:

- A new, pure, representative democracy will bloom. Voting on all issues will take place anytime, anyplace, with weekly deadlines for national roll calls, and **immediate** feedback on polling results.

- Logon for voting will be easily accomplished via use of a password, which will be your Social Security Number. (Boomers, Xers, Millennials: we might as well get **something** out of our 14% salary contributions, right?)

- Training in use of the Internet to vote on issues will be compulsory, beginning in primary school, vastly increasing the technological savvy and American values of our children.

- The cost benefits will be tremendous – does anyone think we can't design an online voting system for less then an annual operating cost of a billion dollars?

- A renaissance of increased citizenship and personal responsibility at the federal level will reinvigorate our Democracy, once again, placing America in a position of leadership, inspiring the world. Just as the innovation of representative democracy was light years ahead of the world of the 1700s, on-line voting by all citizens will place American democracy at the forefront of the world's free nations, the envy of self governing peoples worldwide.

- The People will be a new, active, vigorous legislative body, countering the right, proper, deeper deliberations of the other half of Congress, The Senate.

In closing, bear in mind that our founders never envisioned our current world, where technology truly allows all of the people to be heard, and the formation of a new branch of government, of the people, by the people, for the people, is now possible. Happily, the paradigm of representative Democracy has shifted, we have entered a new epoch for Democracy, and we are alive to enjoy its fruits.

And, as the voters of California have shown, in a rapidly changing economy, people like rapid change. Power holders and incumbents don't like the new reality. Dreamers, ask yourselves this important question: "Which side am I on?"

Caveat / Prediction:
You won't support this innovation if you:

A. Currently sit as a member of Congress

B. Distrust average citizens exercising power for themselves

C. Enjoy costly, noisy, bi-annual elections

D. Loathe the idea of down-sizing government

E. Represent a political party

F. Feel timid about personally making important decisions affecting your life

G. Fear change, hate trying new things, think inside the box, enjoy sitting on the sidelines of life, and can't make decisions

H. Get sweaty palms when using the Internet

I. Love politicians, and feed on politics

J. Enjoy the current system, where your voice is heard federally at a faint 1/690,000th strength

VI - 15-17 Year Old Suffrage

Before the heroism of the women's movement and suffragists, the rights of women to fully share in our Democracy were questioned by the establishment.

Antecedent to the Emancipation Proclamation and subsequent amendments to the Constitution, the rights of African-Americans to fully share in the American Dream were questioned by the majority of American sensibilities.

Prior to the corrective actions of the early 1970s, the birthrights of 18, 19 & 20 year olds to vote were questioned by thinking citizens.

We now know that what was accomplished to further the exercise of full freedoms by Americans was not only right, but righteous; with each successive wave of voting reform, a more perfect union was formed.

The time has come to re-enfranchise our younger citizens, restoring their hopes for better futures, and for those ages 15-17, rewarding these youths for their academic excellence, allowing those whose grade point averages are at 3.5 or above the full voting rights and privileges of participative Democracy.

VII - National Service - AmeriCorps, Peace Corps, The Military

Each American, upon reaching the age of consent and up until the age of 24, will be required to serve their nation for a period of two years in either: a branch of the military, the outstanding AmeriCorps program, or via the Peace Corps.

This service will at once accomplish the spread of Americanism, the inculcation of patriotism, service to our fellow-citizens and global friends, exposure to the reality of life outside these United States, an improved world, and a newly idealized youth. It's just a good, old-fashioned carryover from the days of the New Deal and the draft.

It's plowing time in the field of opportunity for our youth, and the playing field will be leveled between those who are born into wealth and those who are compelled to serve their nation as a means toward advancement. Successful completion of National Service will entitle each citizen to receive a post-secondary education voucher in the amount of $40,000.

Americans have lost touch with the very American ideal of national service.

Dreamers know that once people give of themselves toward the advancement of a cause greater than the self, it's difficult for them to change their mind about it.

We wonder if the support for our current global war against Radical Islamists would be more widely supported if the average American were actually giving of themselves for the war effort. Our military and their families are certainly making the sacrifices, but what of the citizenry?

In World War Two, we sold war bonds to fund the borrowing our government needed to do to produce war materiel. Today, in good economic times, we are borrowing almost $1 billion per day via the sale of treasury bonds. In effect, we are fighting a war to be paid for by our children, and their children.

In World War Two, we had a draft. Today, we extend the rotations of our "volunteer" service members to make up for a lack of personnel. Many enlisted men and women are not pleased with the Defense Secretary's policy of involuntarily extending their duty in Iraq and Afghanistan.

In World War Two, we held aluminum, paper, fat, iron, and rubber collection drives - everybody got involved, from the seniors to the Boy and Girl Scouts.

Think back only to October of 2001, when our President was asked what he wanted the average American to do, in light of the attacks of 9/11. Our Commander in Chief responded, and we quote, "Keep on spending."

We have. The current administration has added more national debt than all others before it, and we deplore this unfortunate milestone.

Dreamers see the differences between the leadership of Franklin Delano Roosevelt and George W. Bush, both in terms of asking the American people for sacrifice, and the call to rediscover the American virtue of national service.

VIII - A National Identification Security System

Before we can hope to eliminate a repeat of the 9/11/01 scenario with all its horrors, we must recognize that the days of paper passports, magnetic diode strips on the backs of 52 different national identifications, personal identification numbers and photo IDs have passed us by. Each of the 19 religious zealot cowards that boarded the 4 airplanes on September 11th, 2001 had passports. Those days are gone. But what system can adequately replace our currently outdated methods?

American Dreamers realized that to effectively control Radical Islam and all the rest of the hate-filled failures of the earth, we needed to seal our borders, establishing a tracking system, equipping each and every shipping container and truck large enough to contain a low-yield nuclear device with radiation emission sensors. The cost? Less than that of two aircraft carriers plus one B-2 bomber. Simply done – yet, these tasks remain unaccomplished by our current government.

American Dreamers realized that to keep cowards from slashing the throats of flight attendants, armed

Air Marshals must be present on each and every flight into or within the United States. That was simple math – yet, the task remains unaccomplished by our current government.

American Dreamers also recognize the desire of some in government to keep out those who would look us in the eye and intend to cause us harm by tracking each and every human being living in or traveling to the United States. These planners envision such systems as unavoidable, and very strict rules governing the use of such prophylactic technologies must be envisioned and firmly entrenched in law before they are presented to us.

Within our lifetimes, we can count on the establishment of a national (and therefore global) identification system that will use existing technologies, will be cheap, and will render diode strips, fingerprints, retina scans, personal identification numbers, holograms, photo IDs, and yes, even chips, all uselessly outdated.

What's coming? DNA encryption implants that not only must be in contact with the living host's live DNA, but that store enough data to tell our complete stories much more efficiently than can any Passport or driver's license. These implants can and will be tracked by location.

Sound crazy? Think again - the technology not only exists, but the cost per implant will be no higher than are our current 52 forms of national identification issued by state DMVs. Biowell Technology, a Taiwanese firm, has already mastered the elements of personal DNA identification and encryption security.

Dreamers, please read about this technology. It cannot be compromised - the moment one removes the implant from its host, it no longer functions.

Additionally, it stores lots of information - much, much more than the current chips used by vets, and by some well intentioned parents, who want to take the arrow of child abduction out of the quiver of the monsters out there, ameliorating their darkest fears.

Americans, do you think that our government would have a hard time selling non-elective surgery to the populace? As a member of the 50% of the population already on the receiving end of such procedures, males do not. After all, as babies, the pain of circumcision was soon forgotten. The potential benefits? Highly ethical.

Dreamers recognize that on September 10th, 2001, you could have **never, ever** sold the sacrifices of liberty fought and died for by hundreds of thousands of Americans in our first 225 years. But you **can** sell it (and cheaply) in the post-9/11 world. Our President did just that, our Congress bought it, and they even had the temerity to call it the "Patriot Act."

Today, you could **never, ever** sell the implant of a DNA encrypted national identification system in the

America we live in. *That's the way it is, and should be.* Dreamers hope and pray that the current reality **never** changes, not only for moral and ethical reasons, but because our vision of the freedom that was America, borne by great minds in Philadelphia, back in 1776, has already been compromised. We may, one day, God willing, return to what once was.

Our darkest fear is that someday, in the not too distant future, when an American city is a smoking, ruined, radioactive crater, some American leader (or despot) will sell us on the next system, doing so in a way that will make the current Administration's tactics and *strategery* look like child's play.

Regrettably, the technology to accomplish this now exists, in the form of DNA identification implants. These strips, and a nationwide system to read them, will eliminate all but the first time offenders.

Future planners will sell us on the fact that that's a reasonable risk, especially with the capability to identify country of origin and history of crime with one swipe. The concept is simple, the technologies already exist, and the time to act against such an involuntary system is now.

Instead, we propose a system which combines lie detection and personal identification, and, for foreign nationals wishing to visit the United States, willing submission to a detailed, thorough background check, vouched by responsible American hosts, featuring no fewer than two visitors in a visiting partnership.

IX - "Gay" Marriage

American Dreamers do not agree that "gay" marriage is ethical.

The purpose of marriage is to seal a covenant with another person under God's approval, at least the God of Christians, Jews, Muslims and Buddhists, and the gods of Hindus, just to name the Big Five.

The purpose of marriage is to produce and rear physically, mentally and emotionally healthy children.

The purpose of having a mother and a father is to rear children in a loving environment that prepares them for success throughout their lives.

If the American civilization is to avoid the fate that has befallen every other great nation that embraced homosexuality before it, from the Abyssinian Caliphate to the Persians to the Greeks to the Carthaginians to the Romans to the Bushido Japanese, "gay" marriage must be avoided.

The great Roman Emperor Marcus Aurelius, a true philosopher and wise stoic, once said, "Men raise their children to be successful. Women raise their children to work in groups. One absent the other is like an arrow without a bow."

Khalil Gibran, author of *The Prophet*, once said, "We are as bows, and our children are as arrows."

We'd better aim high, aim well, and aim carefully, fellow Americans.

We'd also do very well to remember ground zero of the current plague wreaking havoc over our species, spawned by the practitioners of promiscuous lifestyles contemporary Americans now call "gay". Gaetan Dugas and his fellow travelers' unethical, filthy actions have inflicted more pain and misery upon the human condition than Hitler, Stalin and Mao combined, and this pandemic is nowhere near its peak.

"Gay" marriage is unethical if the legitimization of homosexual behavior is a result.

Consider the genesis of AIDS - few holdouts doubt an African origin. That minor point may have been worth arguing 20 years ago, but it's no longer relevant, so we trust Americans to get beyond this argument, to the real issue.

What **is** worth remembering is the behavior that spread AIDS - promiscuous homosexuality practiced by Americans.

In order to cement the rationality of the direct relationship between homosexuality and AIDS, let us examine the research of Traci D. Cocco, excerpted from http://history.acusd.edu/gen/text/aids.html:

"Acquired Immune Deficiency Syndrome was founded in 1976 in Zaire, Africa but was not taken seriously until 1985. The media finally began to pay attention to the deadly disease when actor Rock Hudson passed away from complications caused by the AIDS virus in 1985.

"Though by this time over twelve thousand Americans were either dead or infected with the virus, nobody seemed to take notice. The mass media ignored AIDS until the death tolls were too high to avoid the sensitive topic.

"The media, like the government, felt that America was not ready to cover stories of homosexuals and their sexual behavior. One must wonder if the crisis would be different today if the people had been better informed about AIDS in the early stages of the epidemic.

"The origin of AIDS is quite mysterious to the general public. Ignorant rumors about AIDS have materialized in the last decade, but none are close to the truth. The first reported case of a person to die of complications from the obscure AIDS virus was in 1977. The victim was a Denmark doctor, Margrethe Rask, who was practicing medicine in Kinshasa, Zaire for the past five years. Treating patients in Africa, at this time, was much different compared to current standards. Basic supplies were limited, so gloves were barely worn and needles were reused. It is speculated that Rask became ill through one of her patients via blood.

"By 1980, this unknown African disease reappeared, it had found a way out of the jungle and into the cities (of North America). Doctors of known homosexuals began to notice an increase in a mononucleosis-like syndrome. In many gay patients Pneumocystis Carinii Pneumonia (PCP), an uncommon infection to the lungs, was found which is caused by a problem in the immune system.

"Finally, on June 5, 1981, the Centers for Disease Control (CDC) made its first official announcement on the mysterious disease. In the bulletin, Morbidity and Mortality Weekly Report, five severe pneumonia cases were described. All the cases were found in Los Angeles hospitals. In all of these five patients there were three common qualities found to prove the importance of the warning: the patients were in their twenties, they were homosexuals, and they all had Pneumocystis Carinii Pneumonia.

"According to the CDC report: "The occurrence of pneumocystosis in these five previously healthy individuals without a clinically apparent underlying immunodeficiency is unusual." Could these five patients have had the unknown and deadly AIDS virus? It is quite possible.

"Before that weekly report was written, researchers were trying to locate 'Patient Zero' in 1980. 'Patient Zero' was to play a unique role in the upcoming epidemic. He was found by the Centers for Disease Control and his name was Gaetan Dugas, a French-Canadian airline steward. Many gay men, nationwide, knew of this handsome man in the gay bars and bathhouses, or sex clubs for homosexual men. Dugas was popular among the men because of his charming personality and risky sexual behavior.

"It was in the summer of 1980 that Gaetan Dugas began to notice a rash and purple spots on his face and body. The doctors realized that Dugas had Kaposi's Sarcoma (KS), a form of skin cancer that was later associated with AIDS. Many doctors noticed that Kaposi's Sarcoma was only seen in homosexual men, so it was dubbed the 'gay cancer'. Though this did not stop the sexually active Dugas, he continued to travel to San Francisco, Los Angeles, Vancouver, Toronto, and New York visiting numerous bathhouses.

"Gaetan Dugas was, later, to figure that he had two hundred and fifty sexual contacts a year. In all, Dugas had had two thousand five hundred sexual partners.

"In 1982, after major researching by the Centers for Disease Control, a link was found between Dugas and nineteen gay patients dying from a bizarre condition. Out of those nineteen, Dugas had sex with four of the patients. Another four had gone to bed with people who had had sex with Gaetan Dugas, or 'Patient Zero'.

"Finally, Dugas was told by doctors to stop participating in any sexual activity because he might be transmitting this disease to others. Gaetan Dugas replied to this harsh order, "Somebody gave this thing to me. I'm not going to give up sex." Dugas followed through with his deathly promise and continued to have anonymous sex in the bathhouses. In fact, after having sex with men, Gaetan Dugas would point to his purple lesions caused by the disease and say, "I have the gay cancer. I'm going to die and so are you!"

"At this same time, 1982, a new name was given to the 'gay cancer.' Acquired Immune Deficiency Syndrome (AIDS) was adopted because it was universal and was sexually neutral. The previous name for the syndrome, Gay-Related Immune Deficiency (GRID), was replaced after doctors noticed the virus did not just affect homosexuals.

"Up until 1984, Gaetan Dugas continued to have unprotected sex. On March 30, 1984, Dugas's aggressive behavior was finally put to an end when he died of a disease called AIDS. Whether Gaetan Dugas brought AIDS to the United States....there is no doubt that Gaetan Dugas recklessly spread AIDS throughout the United States.

"Many questions have arisen during the lethal time period of 1980 until 1985 about the fast spread of the AIDS virus. Most Americans wondered why the gay bathhouses were allowed to continue their business when a majority of the clients were infected with AIDS. It was a known fact that the bathhouses around the United States were there for one reason: anonymous sex among men. The bathhouses were a perfect breeding area for the virus but business continued as usual.

"A major controversy emerged about the bathhouses and state power over these clubs. With these businesses operating, it showed that the American public could endure the lifestyle of homosexuals. Thus, when suggestions were brought up to shut the bathhouses down it became a huge debate about government intervention. Public Health officials believed that closing the baths would be a good idea to stop the spread of AIDS. Many gay owners of the bathhouses and gay activists saw the options as a way to contain homosexuality. They were frightened that the shutdowns would not stop there and continue into the gay bars and other gay establishments. Also, the owners of the bathhouses were not going to give up a $100 million industry.

"This type of response is how AIDS was spread so drastically around North America in the early eighties. The gay business owners of the baths were not interested about a deadly disease running rampant through their clubs just as long as they received money from the clients. During these early years, the owners could have been more concerned about the health of their numerous clients instead the owners were just profiting from them. With this type of ignorant behavior, the Director of the Department of Public Health, Dr. Meryvn Silverman finally put an end to the bathhouse controversy.

"On October 9, 1984, Silverman compared the bathhouses to "Russian Roulette parlors". He ordered the closure of fourteen baths that "promote and profit from the spread of AIDS". Silverman continued: "These fourteen establishments are not fostering gay liberations. They are fostering disease and death." Finally, a public official had taken action even though it was four years too late. AIDS was beginning to spread like a brush fire because of inconsiderate profiteers, like some bathhouse owners. By 1985, all the bathhouses in America had been put out of business by the government. These owners lost an incredible amount of money, but almost ten thousand people had already lost their lives to AIDS. "

For more on the subject, we suggest the book, *"And The Band Played On"*.

America must recognize the world-wide attitude that was recently enunciated by a Black, female South African student, speaking out for an entire continent and class of victims. When asked, "Do the majority of South Africans link AIDS to the United States?" Her instant reply was damning in its simplicity: "AIDS is an American export."

To encourage change, America must replace the export of fear, and death, and promiscuous homosexuality with the export of hope. To the Bush Administration's great credit, this effort has begun.

X - Government Spying On Its Own Citizens

Sadly, the only safely secure way remaining for any two human beings to communicate in the 21st Century A.D. is by using two cups and a string, or by flashing sunlight reflections off of obsidian, or perhaps by whispering in the wind, or by signing in a secure area.

Every possible form of communication, from short-wave to microwave, from fishing boat chatter to missile launch synchronization, from board room braggadocio to bedroom banter, *can be* and *is* collected, transmitted, stored, sifted, analyzed and reported upon by our National Security Agency.

With annual defense budgets of $500 Billion (counting our two lingering wars) your NSA falls within the broad parameters of what is called "Black Operations", or the $45 Billion that is spent on things that not every Senator, Representative, or citizen has "need to know" about.

Our NSA has 25,000 employees, and is headquartered in Ft. Meade, Maryland, not too far from the infamous town of Laurel, where George Wallace's presidential candidacy of 1972 was ruthlessly ended by the bullets of Arthur Bremer. Meade was a capable Union General in the War Between the States. The NSA is halfway between Baltimore and Washington, in a beautiful area, quietly nestled just a 2 hour drive from Philly, 1 hour from the Chesapeake, and 3 hours from western Maryland.

If the FBI is Uncle Sam's cop, and the CIA is his cloak and dagger, and the DIA is his librarian, and the DOJ is his judge, and DARPA is his special weapons lab, and the military intelligence branches his tactical operations training grounds, and Ft. Dietrik his poison lab, then the NSA is his ears. Much of the work of these agencies is called "Black Operations". As Americans, we all pay well for it, it is a generally effective team, it scares the hell out of the bad guys, and it missed 19 men on four airplanes in a two hour operation on a late summer morning in 2001.

While eavesdropping is *not* a purely Yankee art, to be sure, the mechanics of the machine collection of intelligence have certainly been mastered by the Americans. Here's how it is supposed to work:

United States Signals Intelligence Directive 18 prohibited the American Spy from willfully collecting any communications between U.S. citizens. Communications originating *in* the continental United States with a *non-U.S.* destination, or communications originating *outside* of CONUS with a *U.S. destination*, with *one or more* party being determined to be a non-U.S.

citizen, are entirely fair game. Every other communication in every other country is fair game. Period, end of story.

Until October of 2001, and the arrival of The "Patriot Act."

Today, average Americans will be astonished to learn what kinds and types of information are now in play for the spies whose salaries our tax dollars pay. This silent sacrifice of freedom is the untold story of the so called Global War On Terror.

Our humble advice for all citizens is to **trust absolutely nothing** to any form of electromagnetic communication; there are no longer any moral compunctions or legal safeguards protecting any American citizens from being declared "persons of interest" in the prosecution of the GWOT.

This is but one by-product of the Bush Administration's *strategery,* and rest assured that Messrs. Franklin, Washington, Hamilton, Jefferson, and Madison must be spinning like tops in their graves, at what has become of the vision that was Freedom, Liberty and Democracy in Philadelphia back in 1776.

The degeneration of freedoms in our constitutional republic in just the few years since 2001 is unprecedented, eclipsing any qualitative measures or comparisons to the degeneration between the reigns of Julius Caesar and Emperor Augustus. We have already spoken to the degeneration of our national wealth in this same time period, as we will soon witness the Congress raising **our** National Debt limit to $8.4 trillion.

The tragedy is, if one mentions these losses of freedoms on talk radio (or in polite conversations) as we have, the vast majority of thinking Americans will shrug, cluck their tongues, sigh, and chalk it up to the reality of "fighting the terrorists". "If you ain't got nothin' to hide, why worry?" goes the simple mantra, from equally simple minds.

Back to the spying - here's how it works.

In the bowels of the NSA www.nsa.gov are an array of Cray Corporation supercomputers, http://www.cray.com/ featuring linear connectivity, with floating magnetic dynamic random access memories, that can perform over 3 trillion calculations **per second**. The room is enormous, and to see it, to hear the droning of its super-coolers, to feel the whoosh of icy air rushing past pants legs, is to feel like one has entered nothing less technologically advanced than the set for the Emperor's lair on Lucas' **Star Wars** Death Star! It is awesome.

Tens of thousands of operatives, perhaps humble and hardworking Chinese linguists, go to work each day, log on to the Cray system, and are queried by their desktop computer for the day's catchment.

What languages would you like?

Chinese and English.

What source and destination territories would you like?

The People's Republic of China and the United States of America.

What timeframes would you like?

1/9/90 to 2/13/91.

What keywords would you like?
(This is the art of the game, because our foreign friends do not often use the actual words referenced.)

Missile, warhead, kryton, yield, detonator, U-238, U-235, uranium, plutonium, re-entry.

Timing parameters? *(This is called the 'sandwich', or the amount of traffic preceding and following the use of the keyword(s) in the conversation. Good intelligence analysts like theirs super-sized.)*

30 seconds before, 60 seconds after.

Thank you, please stand by.

About an hour later, our operative receives a pile of traffic, calls up a detailed map using the very best software that can be purchased in a world of $649.99 toilet seats, carefully plotting the source and destination of each communication, happily building complex puzzles with no box cover.

The best operatives can see the pictures materialize without even solving half of the puzzle. Would that the United States had these experts covering Arabic speaking Middle-Eastern expatriates and student visa holders during the late 1990s and early 2000s.

Fellow Americans, please trust us when we say that *you* and *I* are all now part of the puzzles being assembled.

The point of this all, and the mystery of the "Patriot Act," is that if one likes (and trusts) the current key leadership, one might not have a problem with this system, and being spied on indiscriminately by one's own government, and being subject to consistent intrusions of one's basic individual rights, not the least of which is the right to privacy. In fact, like 52% of Americans today, one might even think it's a good thing - after all, "If you ain't got nothin' to hide...."

The ethical question we must wrestle with, as did the Board of Hewlett Packard, upon learning that it was being spied upon by its leadership, is this: What happens to our trust of this nation's key leadership on the next Inauguration Day, 2009?

Sleep well, "Patriot Act" true believers.

XI - Global Focus - Internet Forums - Cultural Exchanges

No technology in the history of human-kind is as potentially emancipating as that which is offered by the Internet, and global access to the World Wide Web.

American Dreamers recognize the fact that to begin disentangling our nation states, races and peoples from millennia of strife, enmity, jealousy and warfare, the key is to create equality through access to opportunity.

No system offers the ability to link peoples of all races, creeds, religions and ideologies to think globally and act locally better than The Internet.

American Dreamers envision moderated global focus groups, task forces, chat rooms, and action groups, linked via the wonder of text translation software that allows any printed word to be rendered into an audio signal.

Picture a simultaneous world-wide task force on global warming, moderated in Stockholm, with content servers located in Beijing, and participants via tele-conferencing or videoconferencing from across the world as we know it, leap-frogging slow moving or corrupt governmental authorities.

Or, better yet, picture a global focus group debating action plans for aid to victims of natural disasters. The concepts are simple, the technologies already exist, and the time to Dream is now.

XII - The Environment

The conclusive evidence is in – the globe is warming, and mankind's impact on this destructive trend through the production of greenhouse gases must be controlled.

The United States of America, with 3.9% of the world's population, produces 26% of the world's greenhouse gases.

A nation as great as America must not continue to be the largest part of a growing problem; we can do better. The solutions will be simple, but not easy.

1.) Admit the problem

2.) Own the problem.

3.) Cap greenhouse gas emissions.

4.) Decrease the use of fossil fuels.

5.) Seek technologies that can scrub the air of carbon dioxide, and use them.

6.) Lower Co2 levels.

7.) Show the world how a leader should act.

XIII - The Weekly Honor Roll - America's Best On Parade

Each month, exemplars of excellence will be methodically selected and highlighted in the following vital areas:

Fine arts

Sports

Performing arts

The humanities

Physical sciences

Industrial sciences

Leadership

Marketing & salesmanship

Business & entrepreneurship

Spirituality & humanitarianism

Communication & eloquence

Americanism

Bravery

Independence

Each month's nominees will be selected nationally, one vote per citizen. Yearly, the American Excellence Awards will be bestowed upon the very best from amongst the monthly honor rolls, and "average Americans" will enjoy their very own "Oscars," in recognition of real life excellence.

XIV - Freedom From Light Sweet Crude Oil

Their once was a vision that set American foreign policy squarely on the path of bleeding the Middle-East of its light, sweet crude oil, as quickly and as inexpensively as possible. This model resulted in the quagmire that is the war in Iraq, and the run-up to the war on Iran.

This was the old model, no longer applicable in the present days of $60 per barrel oil, Iranian threats to shipping via the Hormuz Straight, the rise of coward terrorist groups like Al Qaida, an expansionist China, and the quagmires of endless Middle-Eastern conflicts.

We must move substantially toward the development and exploitation of our own nation's deep reserves of shale, natural gas, coal, solar, and tidal power. By doing so, we will unshackle ourselves from acting in a part of the world where American interests, American values, and American lives are disrespected.

The Middle-East can hold its oil, while Americans enjoy better uses of our treasures of life, wealth accumulation, and liberty.

Our own energy reserves are vast, will not be exhausted for centuries at current levels of usage, and will result in a boom in American jobs.

XV - The Birthright of Personal Wealth Security

Each American Citizen, at birth, will be entrusted with a $10,000 personal savings entitlement.

Each and every year for the remainder of their lives, each law abiding citizen will accrue an additional 2% of the amount in their personal savings entitlement, added to their Personal Savings Account, until they reach the age of 75, when they may be withdrawn for use.

The monies so invested will be held in trust as national savings equity, invested completely in U.S. Treasury Bonds, earning a modest but consistent rate of return, and raising the national savings rate.

The Personal Savings National Trust, whose assets will be untouchable by The People or the Senate, may eventually serve as a viable alternative to the existing (and bankrupt) Social Security System.

XVI - Cleaning Up After The 20th Century

Earth was insulted by the dawn of the nuclear age, the first halting steps in mankind's use of nuclear power, and experimentations in use of harmful chemicals during the last century.

There is a solution. All spent nuclear fuel, radioactive waste products and toxic chemicals will be rocketed directly to the planet Venus, in an unprecedented abatement project involving thousands of extra-terrestrial missions.

To earn the admiration of future generations, our generation will launch, and will succeed in implementing the largest abatement project in the history of mankind.

This will be accomplished because it must be done, if we are to achieve long-term survival for our species, insuring a lasting legacy for our world.

XVII - Second Languages - Adopted Lands

Nearly every American (even a plurality of our previously dislocated Native American brothers and sisters), in addition to the birthrights of Liberty and the pursuit of happiness, shares in one additional key commonality - we are all nomads, descendants from the very best of the world's entrepreneurs, those who took the risk, had the guts to get on the boat or plane, bravely walking or swimming across the borders, taking a gamble on Freedom.

It is what makes us great as a people, and it is the envy of the world. Our very success honors these risk-takers, but do we celebrate this fact?

What to make of our ancestral homelands, and their languages?

How are we to identify with the legacy of our ancestors, while embracing the present, and preparing for the future?

American Dreamers support a pedagogical construct that teaches language and culture to all students, selected by each learner's family, throughout the student's entire primary through secondary educations.

In this way, our citizenry will at once recapture the historic ties that bind them to the rest of this wondrous world, while acquiring a second language, for-

Dr. Tim Dosemagen

ward positioning young Americans for international service to humankind, global competitiveness, reenergizing the ties that bind us to our brave ancestors, anchoring our heritage.

XVIII - Personal Fitness Partnerships

Our citizenry, especially our nation's youth, suffers from an epidemic of spiritual poverty, emotional insecurity and physical obesity.

American Dreamers support the establishment of a three-pronged approach toward forging strength of mind, body and spirit, through Personal Fitness Partnerships.

These volunteer partnerships, managed through the Department of Health and Human Services, will see each citizen voluntarily matched with one mentor, while, in turn, serving as a mentor to another citizen of their choosing.

This methodology will offer the means through which our nation will, at long last, unite each and every generation in the pursuit of personal excellence.

Forging fit bodies, engaging sharp minds and creating a healthy spirituality, Personal Fitness Partnerships will begin in primary school, lasting for lifetimes.

National guidelines on rigor, curricula, programming suggestions and group activity opportunities will be promulgated and shared. A new national program will be born, one absent the uniforms, insignia, allegiances or ideological remnants of the 19th and 20th Centuries.

XIX - Fair Trade - Bilateral Reciprocity

In 1973, the average income of the American worker stood at $37,000 per year. In the nearly four decades since, average incomes have risen by just a few thousand dollars. More people are working more hours to achieve standards of living that are finally stagnating. We are the busiest generation in American history, working ourselves through a frenzy of activities while sacrificing valuable time that could be better spent rearing our children, pursuing self-improvement activities, and bettering our communities.

In 2007, the United States of America will post a record $750 billion balance of trade deficit. That is the largest transfer of wealth in the history of nations, and with this hemorrhage of dollars, millions of well paying American jobs disappear.

We are exporting our wealth, while we import the work of others.

Our Federal Reserve, the Economists, the Trilateralists and all the merchants of the earth tell us that this system is good for us.

In the case of the trade between the U.S. and just one nation, China, in but one year's time, we send over $5,000 per second more to them than they send to us.

American Dreamers realize that the time has come to even the playing field, locking in fairer exchange rates, ensuring reciprocity of bilateral trade, and ensuring the birthright of economic independence for our children.

Today, the Chinese laugh at our supposed economic independence, realizing that were they to stop using our dollar exports (which we blissfully pay for their cheap wares) to purchase our debt (our billions in borrowing via issuance of treasury bonds), making money from our Federal Reserve (interest paid on the bonds when cashed in), our nation would be brought to its knees in a wave of higher interest rates, higher mortgage rates, accelerated inflation and the collapse of the dollar. They know it, we know it, and they know we know they know it.

So be it – the time has come to call the Great Chinese Bluff – we call for an exchange rate of 4 RMB to one U.S. dollar, and no less.

Best of all – more American jobs will result, with a gradual reduction in the largest line item of our national budget after defense and entitlements – interest on the National Debt.

Enough debt, enough export of the nation's wealth – American Dreamers demand full control of our own national destiny.

XX - Access To Education For All

Following National Service, each American will receive a post-secondary educational voucher in the amount of $40,000.

For those citizens who are "grandfathered" beyond compulsory National Service, no interest student loans will be available, in the amount of $40,000, in the critical fields of education, preventive medicine, engineering, information technology, nanotechnology, biogenetics, and land & water conservation.

Our citizenry will be better educated, and our nation will be forward positioned to meet the challenges of the 21st century.

As a by-product of this educational rewards schema, our colleges might even mint a few thousand less Juris-Doctorates per year, too. Less litigation...more production...a better America.

XXI - Hydrogen, Solar, Tidal, Magnetic and Orbital Power

There exists more potential power in the process of separating oxygen from hydrogen, with existing technologies, than that which exists in all the dead biomass under the sands of a hundred Middle-Easts.

There exists even more energy in the capture of one earth rotation's worth of sunlight, with existing technologies, than that of every power plant on earth operating at full capacity for a week.

There exists even more potential power in capturing the tidal movements and deep currents of the waters covering 70% of our planet's surface.

Finally, drag a 400 mile long electricity collecting tether from the tail end of the Space Shuttle through the ionosphere, and more energy will be collected than can be imagined.

The ultimate American Dream?

Harnessing the potential power of the moon's movement relative to that of earth.

What the mind of man can conceive it will achieve. The time to reach for solutions is now.

Dr. Tim Dosemagen

XXII - SETI

There are over 100,000,000 galaxies in the known universe, each of which holds an average of 100,000,000 stars.

God's true greatness is revealed in the following two questions: Why would we on earth be alone, in all of His vast creation? And, if we were alone, why would we be the only ones to know it?

The time to continue our relentless search for greater glimpses of the glory of this universe has arrived.

Knocking ever louder on the doors of the heavens, the Search for Extraterrestrial Intelligence must be augmented by the American citizenry – anyone with a PC will be encouraged to join forces under the leadership of a new NASA with a bold new mission – probing the lights and sounds of creation with our eyes and ears.

Until our bodies are freed to reach the stars, our minds must be lifted, as one, to reach for them. We have much to potentially learn from other intelligences.

XXIII - The Great Lakes – Southwestern United States Water Project

To continue the rapid, currently unsustainable movement of population from the cold north to the sunny south, we envision the construction of a great aqueduct stretching from Chicago to Las Vegas, draining excess water from the Great Lakes, and quenching the growing thirst of the great American Southwest.

Arizona is now the 10th most populous state in the union, and the center of our population continues to shift to the south and west.

In a grand system of dollars for water, we envision an environmentally safe, regulated interstate transfer of fresh water for dollars, resulting in manageable lake levels in the Midwest, fattened coffers for the Great Lakes states, as well as our good Canadian friends in Ontario and Quebec, fueling the inexorable 21st Century Great American clarion call to "Go West".

In business, follow the money. In human engineering, follow the resources. In American Dreaming, follow the ideas.

XXIV - Open Immigration From East And South Asia

Today, five of the top ten sources for international students lie in Asia. These Chinese, Taiwanese, Korean, Japanese and Indian immigrants are not only the best minds and most eager learners of our current world, a fact of which our advanced industries and applied research consortiums are well aware, but these potential Americans also represent, at once, the hardest working and most over-achieving cohort of the American population.

The immigrant waves of the late 19th Century significantly augmented the American culture, insuring our success in the 20th Century, and it can be argued that, absent another significant wave of immigration in the 21st Century, the United States may fall victim to the stagnation and intellectual flaccidity now being suffered by the Europeans.

Mexico, South and Central America are trends. Worldwide, today there are more overseas Chinese than there are U.S. citizens. If provided the opportunity, these industrious and proud peoples, along with the rest of those who are entrepreneurial enough to escape the suffocating overpopulation of South and

East Asia, will not only come to America, but American values will subsume this most rapidly expanding portion of the world, embracing the trend in shifting global power from the Atlantic to the Pacific.

If we are to thrive as a leading nation, we must transform the opening decades of the 21st Century into the leading edge of a new wave of immigration, drawing on peoples whom wholly embrace and thirst for the American values of wealth accumulation and personal liberty. This is a uniquely American mission, and represents a uniquely global vision.

XXV - On To Mars!

A world awaits us, and it is our destiny to send men to Mars, and bring them back safely. Terra forming our sister world is not only a viable option for our species, but it is our only hope in offering an alternative to life on earth.

Mars once held oceans, and it will hold them again.

Mars once offered a cradle for life, and its cooler, temperate continents beckon us to build a summer home for our species.

If we choose to ignore this opportunity, failing to unite the space faring nations of the earth in a common effort, we will have slouched through one of the greatest moments of evolutionary opportunity our species has been gifted.

Listen to the naysayers – these are the same timid voices that echo in the dust heaps of history, below valiant stories of Magellan and Columbus, Lewis and Clark, Armstrong and Lovell.

The time to go to Mars and beyond is now.

Exploration and expansion defined our nation; let these same values now define our world, and our species.

Ex nihilo nihil fit. Ad Astra!

XXVI - Retirement At 75

Successive waves of immigration alone won't fix the looming problems caused by the beginning waves of Boomer retirements in 2011.

Instead of just more workers earning more money and paying more taxes, what America needs to recognize is the fact that today, we live, eat and breathe better than ever, and that 30 is really 20, 50 is really 40, and 75 is really 65.

To fix Social Security, to keep our workforce productive, to keep our precious older Americans mentally and physically active, and to keep from falling into the European, Japanese and Chinese Abyss of aging populations and dependent elderly economic stagnation, the American Dream Party wholly endorses American retirement at the age of 75, and not a day before.

XXVII - Universal Health Care - Grouping By Lifestyle Choices

It is no longer fair, nor is it economically feasible, to lump together two people into the same insurance risk groups, who differ in lifestyle choices, as well as the threats posed by inherited hereditary maladies.

Why should two Americans, one who smokes, over-eats, drinks excessively and dwells in an air-polluted city, and another who takes excellent care of herself in all respects, living in an environmentally clean region, pay the same for their health insurance?

American Dreamers recognize the fact that to be fair, our health insurance should be both risk-based and risk-assessed. We do this for drivers, and the time has come to do it for the field of medicine.

Secondarily, the current system of rich and middle class citizens paying for the health provision of poor citizens must end, replaced by a voluntary, universal PPO system of access to healthcare for all, means tested, and focused on preparation and prevention of illnesses before they happen. This will be accomplished through mandatory payroll deductions, using one half of the monies which are currently deducted for Social Security.

The American Medical Association's cartel of licensure and approvals must be permanently eliminated, replaced by a nation-wide network of wellness centers, staffed by a cadre of rapidly trained and certified basic medical practitioners.

Lastly, the evil twin incentives of medical and drug industry profits from prolonged illness and chronic care must be replaced with a system of rewards for the establishment of long-term health and healthier lifestyles.

Prepare, prevent, prolong.

XXVIII - The Global War Against Terrorists

Terrorism is a cancer on humankind, insulting its host, threatening our very survival as a species. The invasion of Afghanistan significantly scattered one source of terrorism, Al Qaida, which quickly metastasized to new locations such as Pakistan, Sudan, Iran, the Philippines and Indonesia.

The invasion of Iraq and its subsequent occupation have accomplished exactly what the cancer needs to survive in an ever shrinking, ever modernizing world – recruiting more cells who are willing to commit the ultimate acts of cowardice, destroying themselves and innocents through acts of "martyrdom".

Saddam Hussein, although one of history's greatest failures, was absolutely correct about one thing: World War III is the Mother of All Battles, pitting the values of civilization and wealth accumulation against the values of Radical Islam. Humankind will never revert to the values of the cancer, and instead, must accelerate its inexorable movement toward global unity, equality of the genders, modernization and universal freedoms.

History's march will neither be quickened via more invasions of nation states, nor long-term occupations, nor total hegemonic control by self appointed "World Policemen." Instead, united, worldwide surgical strikes against terror cells must continue apace, augmented by the continuing therapies of freedom of information, freedom of commerce, freedom from hegemony, freedom from hunger and freedom from disease. In this way, the sacrifices of our precious dead and uncounted treasures on the battlefields of World War III will be honored.

The West needs to be ruthless; but just in combating terrorists. We must not debase ourselves to the indiscriminate attacks against civilians that characterizes Radical Islam's tactics. The age of half-measures died with Ramsi Yusef and the blind sheik back in New York 1993. The world has cancer, and it must be eradicated.

It amazes to think that half of thinking Americans and Britons, and a plurality thinking Europeans still do not realize that The West is locked in an existential battle with terrorists.

Perhaps it's the fog of a current stragery that employs 20th Century tactics, using machetes and hacksaws to fight cancer. Or, perhaps it's the times we live in, and the distractions we all have in a noisy popular culture. Or, perhaps the destruction of two zip codes, with over 3,000 casualties, and a 2% dent in a (then) $11 trillion dollar economy wasn't enough to jar Americans. Or, worst of all, perhaps The West is drunk, distracted, in debt, and fiddling.

We *must* do better, and *shall*.

1. **Seal the borders, keeping the cancer out**. This will never be perfect, but it will work best. The current efforts have sadly left this unaccomplished. Canada and Mexico are porous, and so are our borders with these neighbors. We must do more.

2. **Kill the cancer where it exists**. Afghanistan was smart and effective. Iraq had a malignant narcissist (and sons) in power, and a small element of Ansar el-Islam active in the northeast - these are now gone, America could have and should have withdrawn immediately after flushing this human offal down the toilet bowl of human history. Waziristan should have been, and must be the next stop - it's where OBL lives - we know it, and so does Pakistan's leadership. Yet we have not gone there.

3. **Prevent the cancer from metastasizing**. The "Global War On Terror" has clearly failed here. Egypt's Mubarak said it best - "Occupying Iraq will create a thousand Bin Ladens." Our continuing presence in Iraq, even with noble, worthy objectives we all can agree upon, is exactly what Bin Laden needed to prove to the wider Arab street the so-called intentions of the "corrupt infidels" - land and wealth.

America was snookered, and the ranks of the radicals have grown exponentially. This is the truth that should keep Americans up at night, especially in a day and age with Pakistan just one overthrown military dictatorship away from becoming a purely radicalized "Islamic Republic". Pakistan has 70 - 80 nuclear bombs, the portable kind, some with midrange yields. Pakistan is the key - and there is no coincidence that Bin Laden is there, waiting, planning. Yet, America now engages in a run up to war with Iran, a basket case Islamic Republic that is still years away from possession of nuclear weaponry.

4. **Prevent future instances of the cancer**. This is the "hearts and minds" part of the effort that is unwinnable in light of the growing intolerance and lack of opportunity for the average Muslim, even in oil rich states. The age of oil, for all it was worth, is nearing an end - and the Arab street knows this. Sadly, the only hope for a true reform of Islam, for a true self examination by Muslims of the harmful effects of exporting poisoned minds, will be the same measures brought to bear on Imperial Japan and Nazi Germany in the early 1940s. Smart Muslims get this – radical Muslims say "Bring it on!"

American Dreamers pray that it will not come to this, and yet, wonder why the American government has not publicly stated a policy of Mutually Assured Destruction, should one of The West's great cities be destroyed. What would be less ethical - publicly stating that if New York is smoked, Qom, Teheran, Riyadh and Mecca will be immediately retaliated against, or, doing it after the fact, without warning?

David Ben Gurion once said that, "Courage is a special kind of knowledge; the knowledge of how to fear what ought to be feared and how not to fear what ought not to be feared."

In its prosecution of The Global War On Terror, the United States has, thus far, fallen into the extremists' trap. We are smarter, and better than these terrorists, and must avoid falling into the carefully laid traps of such swine.

In middle 2006, Vice President Richard Cheney, on NBC's Meet The Press television political forum, admitted that 9/11 and the current War in Iraq were unconnected. Dreamers were not surprised to hear him say it - he knew it all along, and so did we. But that's beside the point.

As for the quote from Ben Gurion – he stated it long before he became a hard-line ideologue, and it took years of incessant attacks from Israel's neighbors for his idealism to come to a wiser, sadder, reality-based realization, that sometimes, the enemy is insane.

Perhaps a retired U.S. Air Force Colonel, fighter pilot, and Air Force Academy graduate said it best. In paraphrasing him, he said that he once discovered to his great dismay that he had a nest of killer bees in his back yard. The exterminator said, "You can't fight 'em. You can't persuade them. You can't wonder why they came to your house. You can't act like 'em. All you can do is kill 'em."

American Dreamers recognize the analogy clearly.

XXIX - The Global War Against Terrorists: Methodology

Al Qaida and all other forms of terror are a cancer upon civilization, and must be utterly and ruthlessly destroyed. The West entered World War Three on September 11th, 2001, and chose to fight the cancer exactly where most of it was located: Afghanistan. Dreamers support this cause, and fully support the freedom and continuing economic support of a liberated Afghanistan.

Although small elements of Ansar El-Islam existed in the far north of Iraq prior to the American invasion of that nation in 2003, and although Saddam Hussein terrorized the Kuwaitis, terrorized the Israelis and abused his own populace for decades, we do not agree that Iraq's liberation and subsequent occupation meet the mission requirements of the Global War on Terrorists.

We have had mission creep – from removing Saddam to eliminating WMD to establishing Democracy. As the horror shows of Falluja and Baghdad have demonstrated, just as was the case in South Vietnam, an occupying force cannot, nor will not defeat an organized insurgency unless the local citizenry wants Democracy for themselves more than we want Democracy for them.

More importantly, by occupying Iraq, we have taken our eyes off the true objective, as our British, Spanish, Thai, Indian, Israeli, Dutch and Indonesian friends have sadly discovered for themselves: Radical Islam, the enemy of civilization.

In actuality, civilization has yet to awaken to the realities of World War Three. After the attacks on Washington and New York on 9/11/01, in effect, the United States turned the other cheek. We are a good nation. We also are the most dangerous nation on earth, once provoked to wrath.

To avoid further acts of terror from cowards who choose the easy way out, avoiding the trials, lessons and compromises of life by killing others along with themselves, Dreamers support the re-establishment of an old relic of the Cold War: Mutually Assured Destruction.

If the United States is attacked, any nation-state that is known to provide safe harbor, give comfort to, or otherwise support the causes of international terror (Iran, Syria, Sudan, Somalia, Saudi Arabia) will be immediately retaliated against in a reciprocal manner. If an American city is bombed by Radical Islam, Teheran, Damascus, Khartoum, Mogadishu and Riyadh will be immediately bombed.

If an American city is destroyed via the use of fissile bomb-making material from rogue states such as North Korea, Pyongyang will be immediately eliminated.

Other civilized nations are encouraged to set their own tolerances; Dreamers wish to leave the affairs of our allies to their own doing. The difference between Americans and the cancer is clear: We will only destroy if attacked, and we freely and openly announce our retaliatory intentions, hoping to avoid them. Phase two of the Global War On Terror has begun – precision elimination of the sources of the cancer.

If we fail to eliminate the cancer now, the future is very dark, indeed. The question on the table is: With Al-Qaeda seeking chemical, nuclear and biological weapons, and the likelihood being that, once acquired, these will be used on The West, with the certainty of The West's retribution, the citizens of the world have come to realize that mankind may have finally reached the point in its evolution when war truly <u>cannot</u> be won, only survived.

Because conflict is often destructive, and perhaps because conflict resolution is both fraught with risk and highly time consuming, the art of the game for our species' survival has unfortunately been to place a high value on avoiding conflict. This is the old model.

If anything, one of the lasting lessons of our Modern Age, with its increasing globalization, interdependence and connectivity, will be to embrace conflict before it becomes destructive, especially because our world is becoming more dangerous.

In my novel Prodigies – A Warring Species and the Human Heart, I examine the nature of conflict, and the increasing dangers posed to humankind by an outdated model of conflict resolution, warfare, in the Modern Age.

"To a certain degree, to make war is advantageous. For instance, when one is attacked, or when one's freedom is at risk, or when a threat exists that is so great, it must be preemptively dealt a fatal blow. For centuries, this has been the stuff that turns the pages of history books. Most of the time, at least from our limited perspective, since the winner invariably gets the last say, the morally superior side has seemingly won the war. War provides the combatants with righteous causes, adding perceived value to one's existence. Or, during hard times, war can be a useful distraction.

"Some consider war to be natural. Indeed, one look around us provides countless examples of warfare in nature. Recognizing our evolutionary past, one can quickly draw the conclusion that mankind has been bred for warfare. The fight or flight reaction to threats, our body's ability to produce adrenalin, and the defensive emotion of rage - all serving to protect and preserve us, time and time again. All contributing to war.

"Thus far, these properties have served us well, at least to the extent that one man's rage could bring him to pick up a rock and bash in the head of his enemy, thus saving his life, or keeping his family together, and perhaps, insuring his legacy.

"But at what point does a disposition to war cease being an asset, becoming a liability? When is the warrior spirit no longer beneficial to us? Clearly, in our modern age, things are changing, and technology has rendered total warfare too dangerous for our long-term survival. Access to weapons of mass destruction by individuals in small groups – let alone governments, has grown. These weapons provide instant power to those who are otherwise powerless, the marginalized, the discontented, or the failures of the world.

"So how then, should we deal with our warlike nature under these new circumstances?

"The trend is not good. Yesterday, 19 religious zealots, in the ultimate act of cowardice, crashed four airplanes, taking 3,000 lives with them. Tomorrow, one madman with a nuclear bomb may destroy millions, leading to a cataclysmic cycle of destruction.

"What will be the ultimate answer to the warlike nature and fickle cruelty of the human heart?

"Will our warring species survive to find out?

The question on the table is: With Al-Qaeda seeking chemical, nuclear and biological weapons, and the likelihood being that these will be used on The West, with the certainty of The West's retribution, have we finally reached the point in our evolution when war truly <u>cannot</u> be won, only survived?

If so, God help us to learn to live with the cancer, because only He can.

XXX - Abortion

Although abhorrent and dreadful, in certain situations, abortion may offer the best solution.

American Dreamers recognize that Life begins at the moment sperm and egg form zygote. Sustainable life, however, begins at the 5th month of pregnancy.

Abortion is the choice of the mother and the father.

Notwithstanding incest and rape, before a child is allowed to be killed, both parents should completely agree on taking such action. It's a woman's right – and a man's.

XXXI - Euthanasia

American Dreamers believe that as thinking persons, entirely responsible for our own lives, it is our right and responsibility to decide when, where and how we will die.

30% of us will die peacefully in our sleep; leaving 70% of us other exit modes, some of these painful, hopeless, and tragic. Euthanasia offers personal options that are more ethical than a lingering, agonizing departure from this world as we know it.

Our right to choose death's date, locale and venue is no one else's save The Creator's, unless we or our legal designee assumes the burden of decision-making in this fundamental human right. Death is a private affair.

We favor voluntary euthanasia. We oppose any other form, especially the macabre, disgusting horror show paraded before America and the world during the Clinton years by "Dr." Jack Kevorkian.

XXXII - Alternative Life-styles

An American's sexuality is their personal choice, and it is wholly un-American for one citizen to thrust one's lifestyle upon another, especially when injecting these issues into the mainstream of America's youthful cohorts.

Americans do not care to know the sexual orientation of others, and as such, do not cotton to the parade of alternatives currently in vogue throughout our media, and in some of our larger metropolitan areas.

Human sexuality is a personal issue, and Dreamers believe that it should be so maintained, avoiding the over-intellectualization of so trivial a facet of the total human experience. Dreamers also acknowledge that same sex marriage is not a long-term strategy for the survival and growth of the nation.

Furthermore, Dreamers acknowledge that homosexuality and bi-sexuality are, by their very natures, extremely promiscuous lifestyle choices; thus, in an age of deadly sexually transmitted diseases, and global, sexually transmitted plagues, do not constitute a long-term strategy for the health and well-being of the nation's citizenry.

A message to the Homosexual/Bisexual: Don't tell, and Dreamers won't ask, because we don't care to know.

XXXIII - Sex Offenders National Registry

The monstrosity of sex offenses, especially those perpetrated adult upon child, requires society to treat such harms above and beyond almost all other crimes against humanity.

Today, modern law enforcement techniques now include a scrape of inner cheek skin from every incarcerated person, for inclusion in a nationwide DNA database maintained by each and every one of America's "crossbars hotels", one of modern America's true growth industries.

The FBI and DOJ maintain (and share) a national database of convicted child sex offenders. These lists are used extensively by the Boy Scout organization, and in many cases, have prevented convicted offenders from gaining access to youth.

Dreamers recognize that not only should the child sex offender database be widened to include all sex offenders, but that this database should also be made available, nationally, with its own web presence.

The crime prevention eventualities to be realized by such an actions, as well as the cumulative benefit to the society in lives preserved and protected, renders post-prison sex offender registration not only logical, but moral.

We **do not** agree with the "Oprah Winfrey Bill", a silly knee-jerk effort to mandate fingerprinting and registration of any and all adult volunteers in youth-serving organizations, including the parents of children playing soccer, or joining the Boy / Girl Scouts.

Why? Research finds that 96.6% of all adult on youth sex offenses were perpetrated by first time offenders, largely comprised of homosexual men.

The problems with such fingerprinting systems transcend simple analyses of the preponderance of offenses being perpetrated by first-timers, which is true enough.

The problem with The Oprah Winfrey Bill, and many other proposals from minds equally simple, relates to finances.

Consider the Boy Scout organization, which has 6 million members, one million of which are adult volunteers. If requiring fingerprinting for only the adults, at $15 a per registration, the system would quickly break the financial back of the organization. And that's just one organization.

Portable printing machines, print storage and transmission software, and the tracking system for youth-serving organizations would constitute an entirely new federal bureaucracy. That's frightening enough, because if there's one thing that politicians absolutely adore, its bigger government.

Furthermore, youth-on-youth abuse is 9.5 times more prevalent in Scouting than is that of adult-on-youth. Think about the ethics of this, for just a moment. If we fingerprint, and if we recognize the existing reality of potential abusers, and if we are ethical, then we must fingerprint **all** members, for they are **all** potential offenders.

Now the price tag just quintupled, and for the 6 million member Boy Scouts, at $15 per registry, start up costs would approach $100,000,000, and an additional $15,000,00 per year, since a million members join (and quit) annually.

Maybe Oprah's got that kind of money, but youth-serving organizations trying to train our children in values do not.

XXXIV - The Media

Dreamers recognize the fact that The Media is like a fire – potentially useful if carefully applied, and also capable of causing great harm.

The 1st Amendment to the Constitution guarantees free speech as the birthright of every American, and we concur with the founders. Yet, we also agree that the prating fool who screams "Fire!" in a packed theater represents a clear and present danger to the citizenry.

At its best, The Media educates, entertains, informs, and unites Americans.

To frame the media in its proper perspective, Americans need think back only as far as the run-up to war with Iraq, as the American citizenry was sold, indeed, overwhelmingly convinced, that the war was in the best interests of both our nation and the Iraqi people.

We are certain that President Bush shared in such a conviction back in late 2002 and early 2003, and needed compelling evidence to justify the looming expense in material and manpower that this war was going to cost the nation.

He did not ask for all the truth.

Instead, he directed his CIA Director to give him data that supported the run-up. We got what he asked for – roving biological labs, yellow-cake uranium shipments traced to Niger, and all the worst intelligence that can be expected.

The Media, as the fourth branch of our government, complied in the promulgation of these untruths.

This is the essence of telling the truth with truths that are convenient. Politicos are master craftsmen at this, and what the heck, as long as you *win*, nobody really cares!

At its worst, The Media insults, The Media dumbs down, coarsens, exploitains, and tells 50% of 100% of the truth.

Dreamers admire those contributors to the best of The Media, and castigate those who represent the basest displays of humanity. It's ultimately the choices each and every thinking American must choose to make, each and every day

Do we watch Howard Stern? Or, do we want to improve as human beings?

XXXV - Americanism

The Adopted Lands program proposed by the American Dream Party is one side of a great looking glass for our nation's youth; Dreamers also recognize the demand for the inculcation of a deep knowledge and appreciation of what it means to be American.

In a day and age when trillions of mathematical computations can be performed simply and swiftly with the use of a calculator, there need be no less emphasis placed upon the instruction of mathematics than that which must be placed upon a sound knowledge of the origins and distinctive features of our national birthrights as Americans.

What is it that defines us as a nation?

While freedom from religious persecution launched the Great American experiment, we must recognize the addition of many more arrows to the ever growing American quiver, transforming our great nation into the shining beacon of the world, as enunciated by Presidents John Fitzgerald Kennedy and Ronald Wilson Reagan.

Led by the outstanding Library of Congress, and working in tandem with the Smithsonian Institution, Dreamers envision the creation of a web-based American Tutorial, a compendium of vignettes on the lives of thousands of distinguished Americans, reconstructing hundreds of defining moments in our history, and, of course, featuring the recipients of the American Excellence Awards.

Youngsters will be rewarded for successful completion of the American Tutorial's unique set of interactive activities, as they climb the ladder of American awareness from a poverty of ignorance, rising step-by-step, from heroes to entrepreneurs, lesson by lesson, climbing through a colloquium of lifetimes, amidst a carefully guided inculcation of American values, toward the top rung of a rock-solid awareness of American events, American innovations, American contributions to humanity and the human condition, American bravery, valor and courage, leading to an ultimate awareness of the American birthrights of greatness and world leadership.

Culture is to patriotism as personality is to individualism. During the 20th Century, far too much emphasis was placed upon the entertainment oriented aspects of American Culture.

Dreamers recognize and embrace the need to shift the national zeitgeist from one of gaudy navel gazing and loud bling to one of recognition of excellence.

Through the American Tutorial, a great nation will do just that.

XXXVI - The International Library of Lifetimes

For eons, the only legacies a person could hope to leave behind as lasting contributions to the human condition were genes (descendants), memes (ideas and culture) and wealth (property and money).

Yet, if true love is simply the deep act of unconditional sharing, what can humankind lovingly share with its great-grandchildren, beyond the ephemeral? What really lasts, unlike the accumulations of wealth (which may be looted), the collections of lands (which may be usurped), the spread of ideas (which may be perverted), and the lines of clans (which may be annihilated)?

Thankfully, we now dwell within an age where, for the very first time in human history, the technology now exists to allow each and every desiring American the opportunity to easily and effectively leave a lasting legacy, one transcending the physical, embracing the spirit.

The American Dream Party advocates the creation of the International Library of Lifetimes, a global database of home-made, personally created multi-media records of the lives and times of people, administered

---

by the United Nations. Interested persons may elect to logon to the Library of Lifetimes, adding data as they wish, to a permanently maintained database. Question prompts for each entry into the Library shall include, but will not be limited to:

When and where were you born?
What was your childhood like?
What advice would you most like to share with children?
What was the best thing your parents did for you?
What is the value of hard work?
What is the secret to success?
What is your best memory?
What worries you the most?
What is the comparative value of wealth in life?
What do you think pleases The Creator the most in humanity?
What do you think displeases The Creator the most in humanity?
Who is your favorite role-model, and why?
What is your greatest achievement?
What is your greatest disappointment?
If you could live forever, would you?
If you could ask The Creator one question, what would it be?

The data so collected and made available to any interested persons via the International Library of Lifetimes, shall be held in perpetual trust, treated as a shared global resource, protected from the changing winds of politics and alliances, creating a lasting legacy of the accumulation of lives to civilization, and the evolution of the human condition. The time to dream is now, fellow travelers.

XXXVII - Post-Polio Eradication: The Power Of United Service To Humanity
The Next Disease Targeted For Elimination: AIDS

Rotary International, a global organization born in 1905 in a small room in Chicago, adopted the eradication of polio as its global emphasis over two decades ago.

Today, in combination with the good efforts of the U.N. and federal governments world-wide, Rotarians have traveled the globe, contributing hundreds of millions of dollars and millions of hours toward the elimination of the scourge of polio.

Today, the Western Hemisphere is clear of this killer, while tomorrow, complete elimination of the disease is realistically anticipated.

If a service club with a membership of just over a million can accomplish so great a feat, and we must salute all Rotarians for having so done, what could this generation, united in effort, accomplish in our lifetimes?

The American Dream Party of the United States boldly proposes the complete eradication of the entire family of human immunodeficiency viruses, beginning with HIV-1, HIV-2, and HIV-3.

While Dreamers embrace this great effort out of a sense of noblesse oblige, to be sure, with over 100,000,000 people now carrying these viruses and over 45,000,000 men, women and children having needlessly died, if we are to thrive as a species, simple self-preservation demands no less.

XXXVIII - Animals & Shared Nature

Jennifer Hager, in a moving, sensitive treatise, once wrote: "My concept is this: beliefs shape values, which shape morals, which form ethics. I believe that animals are God's creation and His creatures. This belief shapes my value of animals as fun, interesting, comforting and instructional. My value of animals leads me to a moral decision about my behavior towards them; I respect animals and make an effort to look at animals as contributors to my world."

How evocative and powerful this is. Who couldn't see the design of The Creator in the eyes of a walrus, silly as he may seem? Or, the smile of a Labrador Retriever, or, for that matter, the red fox running by the river?

American Dreamers are all about the protection of natural habit, the preservation of all life, a respect for humankind's co-inhabitants, and policies that insure the continuing health, safety, security, and long term survival of the biosphere and its inhabitants.

If we are to survive as a people, then we must protect our home, the earth.

XXXIX - Legalization & Government Controlled Drug Trade

Jack Tirrell once wisely mused that "If the government were to take over the drug business (including currently illegal substances) I would oppose it on grounds that because "recreational" drugs have an impairment aspect, the government would then become the substitute for the neighborhood "pusher." I believe this would be unethical."

Think back to the American CIA's ham-handed fundraising schemes in Southeast Asia back in the 1960s and early 1970s, and return of the record opium exports by the U.S. protectorate in post-Taliban Afghanistan.

What an unmatched lack of morals those authorities who sanctioned these drug trades demonstrated in SE Asia, and demonstrate now, in spades.

Question: Is "recreational" drug use by individuals OK?

Not if the drugs used are illegal to possess, and / or are illegally produced, gained or gotten.

Question: Is a societal invasion of privacy to stop recreational drug use unethical, or not?

It is not unethical, if society's enforcement of the law follows the proper guidelines for surveillance, interdiction, search and seizure. It is unethical, if the contrived traps often used by lazy law enforcement officials to "catch" perpetrators are used. Entrapment is immoral, represents law enforcement at its very worst, and makes for compelling TV at best.

Question: Is there an ethical difference in the type or amount of drug, or time of usage?

Think of the difference between the commuter train engineer who used marijuana, leading to the awful Baltimore to Washington wreck in the mid 1980s, in comparison with the thousands of over the road truck drivers, on the road as you read these words, high beyond belief, on a steady cocktail of nicotine, caffeine, and No-Doze.

Question: Does drug testing in the workplace for use, not impairment, violate the expectation of privacy?

It does not, because the lingering effects of certain substances obviate making any distinctions between past use and current condition. The degree of impairment is the key - and employers are usually safe if they use workplace safety as the driving wedge for testing - not invading privacy.

Question: **Would it be "ethical" for the government to take over the drug business and sell drugs, thereby taking the profit motive out of selling drugs?**

This panacea always sounds sexy, and to The Taxman, juicy. Dreamers do not think it would be ethical, and here is why:

Legalized gambling is a high growth industry that is wreaking havoc amongst the estimated 10% of the American population that is predisposed toward a harmful habituation of participating in games of chance.

Although it may be humorous (and an odd, ironic, poetic justice) that Brokaw's "Greatest Generation" now proudly constitutes our nation's largest fritterers of discretionary wealth through gambling, we find it morally repugnant (and tragic) that gambling venues such as "Lotto" are a cruel chimera, and slow tax on the poor.

Yet, the government sold "Lotto" as a way to raise easy money for the schools, didn't it? "Me" voted it in. One wonders how the same politicos would sell the benefits of legalized, state-controlled drug trades? The thought frightens.

XL - Downsizing

Yes, downsizing **is** ethical, and represents a natural law of organizational behavior in a competitive market economy.

Just like people, organizations gain weight, get fat, and oftentimes, need to go on a diet. This is a natural process.

The crux of the question, and the nexus between downsizing and ethics is best found in a closer examination of **how** organizations choose to downsize.

We have worked for firms that simply gave people two weeks notice and fired them, ushering employees out the door on a Friday morning at 7:30, after allowing one hour to clear the desk, with security guards at each elbow. We find this practice to be at once distasteful and unethical.

We have also worked for firms that downsized by attrition, carefully waiting to reallocate work once people decided to leave, or were promoted to other positions. We find this practice to be both ethical and efficacious.

The United States military downsized between May, 1945 and the outbreak of hostilities on the Korean Peninsula in June of 1950. While the downsizing was warranted by the stunning achievements of the defeat of Nazi Germany and Imperial Japan, history has shown that this downsizing was excessive, and cost many American lives at the outset of the Korean War.

Therefore, downsizing has many shades of grey, subtleties, and mitigating considerations.

To Dreamers, the most unethical downsizing in history is taking place right now in the People's Republic of China.

At the very same time that Chinese factories are producing record quantities of goods, the Communist leadership is shedding state-owned industries in an effort to ramp up for the competitive mandates being implemented as a result of accession to the World Trade Organization, while encouraging the exploitation of cheap country laborers who are shipped, like chattel, into and out of the eastern cities, where they are disenfranchised.

There are already 150 million partially employed or unemployed workers in the PRC, with more being added by the day.

The instability this represents is a great danger to the long-term stability of China, and yearly workers' uprisings now number in the high thousands, squelched by a fearful shell government run by privileged Beijing-based "Communists."

Yet, the government champions itself as the Chinese Peoples' workers party, espousing "socialist" values to an ever-growing idle labor pool whose lives are being ruined at worst, and whose labors are being exploited at best.

Downsizing Chinese style – never in America.

Dreamers envision moral and conscientious personnel decisions, as befits the most productive workforce on earth.

XLI - Taxation

Graduated income tax scales, tax loopholes, itemized deductions, massive taxation bureaucracies – these are the vestiges of a dark past.

The American Dream Party advocates for the creation of one progressive flat tax on consumption, equally applied to all Americans, regardless of income, irrespective of means, and absent the prejudices of wealth redistribution.

To balance the national budgets of the 2010s and 2020s, we anticipate a flat tax rate of no more than 21%.

XLII - U.S. Business Operating Abroad

American businesses are hereby placed on notice – your patriotism will now be measured in direct proportion to the percentage of all employees that are employed domestically by your firm.

If we are to survive as a global power, the American nation must be about more than the export of jobs, dollars, and debt.

U.S. companies should abide by local laws when doing business in other countries, and this should be stipulated in any and all contracts involving non-U.S. based partners. To be sure, morally and ethically, consideration should be given to the humane treatment of workers, but *within* local laws.

This question has an interesting double edge, and deserves a twist: Many European countries have significantly more comprehensive workers' childcare policies than those enjoyed by we Americans. Europeans reared in a sea of Socialism, look with disdain at the barbarity of American benefits, from vacation days to paid time off to sick days to medical care coverage - the list goes on, and on, and on.

Consider only France's so-called benefits - Sacre bleu! Would we Americans want such workplace ethical values (save economic balls and chains) foisted upon our economy? Never! Americans Dreamers truthfully and correctly argue that the level of support systems in place within worker-friendly, Socialist European societies has actually resulted in lower rates of overall economic growth, and sclerotic workforce mobility.

As we see it, like water - if poured into a terrarium, it will seek and find its own level. It must because, in time, water can do no less. Workers, if poured into an economy, will seek and find their comfort zones in workplaces.

This is an undeniable market force - and puts businesses on notice to make themselves attractive to their existing and potential human capital.

In the early 21st Century, the United States is in a *very* unusual position, when examined historically. We are a *net importer* of workers, and a *net exporter* of positions for overseas workers. Dreamers know that this condition will not last, and will either be corrected by market forces outside of our control, or by concerned citizens who properly and responsibly seize their own destinies.

In a day and age when we are running annual current account deficits of over $700 Billion, the flood of dollars running from the our shores will halt, only via fairer exchange rates, a more level playing field for all global business players, and the expansion of American businesses operating abroad, not through the export of manufacturing and service related jobs, but through the expansion of American products and services from our shores.

XLIII - U.S. Involvement In Iraq

The U.S.'s current involvement in Iraq (since the invasion of 2003) has come to be framed by the current leadership as follows: "The consequences of leaving things only partially achieved will result in much greater danger in the future."

This gets to the essence of the matter quite well. Should U.S. troops remain in Iraq, or be withdrawn? This question requires a deontological examination.

If we invaded to find and destroy WMD, then we have achieved a smashing success. We found shells with traces of chemical agents, and we found and eliminated Baathist Iraq's three most dangerous weapons of mass destruction - Saddam, Uday and Qusai. *Mission accomplished* - bring the fighting men and women home.

If we invaded to topple Saddam - once again, *mission accomplished* - bring our fighting men and women home.

If we invaded to establish Democracy - two nation-wide elections have been held, the Parliament has been elected, the Iraqi Cabinet is in place, and the Key leaders are now representing their Sunni, Shia and Kurd constituencies. Once again, mission accomplished - bring the American ladies and gentlemen home.

Yet - we stay. Why do you think that might be?

Take a quick look at a world map, coloring in the two nations of Iraq and Afghanistan. Look between these two puzzle pieces - Does a picture begin to appear?

Democrats say "It's all about Big Oil!" or, "It's Bush's personal vendetta!"

Republicans say, "We must insure a peaceful assumption of power by the Iraqi Government!" or, "We need to insure Democracy takes root!"

It's all beside the point.

Colin Powell's so-called Powell Doctrine, widely acknowledged and admired on both sides of the political aisles up until the current war, cautioned us to avoid what he termed, 'mission creep'. Actually, he borrowed the concept from H. Norman Schwarzkopf – who built key elements of his philosophy off of the so-called Weinberger Doctrine of the Reagan Administration during the 1980s, but let us not digress.

Think about the objectives of the current U.S. involvement in Iraq, and how these have morphed. Could you imagine doing this in business and getting away with it? Colin Powell walked away from this Administration. He was honest, and ethical. He got burned playing fast and loose with Tenet's Intelligence Directorate's facts on the floor of the U.N. It personally embarrassed him. Dreamers admire him for his ethical behavior.

Interestingly, the Iraqis have been polled extensively on the subject, and overwhelming percentages, when asked the question in red from above, in poll after poll, time and again, have clearly stated: "Thank you very much, now get out."

If these polls are to be believed, and the current U.S. involvement in Iraq is *really* about helping the Iraqi peoples' voices to finally be heard, then why are we *really* staying?

The Iraqi polls say it all - otherwise, United States forces would not have had to destroy Falluja to "save it" - the locals would've kept out the bad guys.

Sunnis don't want Democracy as much as we want Sunnis to want Democracy. This is the same problem America had in S.E. Asia - they called what happened in Falluja "pacification" back then. Colin Powell and H. Norman Schwarzkopf cut their teeth there.

American Dreamers do not want to ask the question, "Should U.S. troops remain in Iraq, or be withdrawn?" again in two weeks, two months, two years, or two decades.

Conservative Republicrats say, "We must not cut and run!"

American Dreamers realize that, as far as our current involvement in Iraq is concerned, we must not linger and bleed.

The Iraqis have spoken – let us do what is morally correct, and obey their wishes.

Historians can argue the causations of any resultant civil wars between Sunnis, Shia and Kurds, in the Ottoman Empire's remnants, picked out of the desert by the British Imperialists of the 20th Century.

Dreamers recognize that whatever were the motives of the American Leadership back in 2003, Iraq is now in the grips of a sectarian civil war. This is the fight of the Iraqis, not the (current) 2 American fighters per day now dying to police a civil war.

The Bush Presidency mis-reached via the occupation of Iraq following the 2003 invasion. A mature citizenry knows when it must adjust its strategy. A stubborn leadership clings to an outdated strategery.

History may yet laud the U.S. for trying to inject Democracy into the beating heart of Islam. History will not long remember the date U.S.'s leaders realized that Islam rejected the Iraqi dosage. Dreamers recognize the rejection.

The outcome of this war is currently in great doubt. American sacrifices in dead, maimed, and dollars spent are being put to the ultimate test.

History will ask: Did the U.S., against all odds, against world opinion, and yes, against original intentions, manage to successfully establish a government of the people, by the people, and for the people, exactly where the well intentioned had always claimed it was impossible?

Our hope is that some day, not too long from now, George W. Bush might share an ironic place in history with Abraham Lincoln, over the issue of waging an unpopular war in a divided country, and over original intentions vs. actual results.

As Lincoln learned so well in transforming a national cause from one of maintaining union to ending slavery, transformational leaders can make the best of a mistake or two - as long as they move the organization (and the world) toward what is in the right.

The reality, as seen daily in the headlines coming from Iraq, is that the United States has unleashed a sectarian civil war that is rapidly leading to the devolution of the former state of Iraq, leading to the establishment of three de facto states.

We now watch as the finest fighting force in the world devolves from liberators to street cops, officiating

Dr. Tim Dosemagen

amongst peoples who despise our presence, abhor our values, and welcome our death.

Out of Iraq, and back to the fight.

XLIV - The Post - John Paul II Roman Catholic Church

In 2006, Pope Benedict, leader of the largest religious organization in the world, criticized Islam in a speech delivered in his home country.

Why would the CEO / Executive Director of a very large religious group go out of his way to criticize members of the next largest religious group? Might his actions have been demographics driven? A deeper analysis is perhaps in order.

We hazard to guess that Benedict gets the state of current affairs, as a pragmatist.

He has inherited a global church that, after being #1 in membership for centuries, is soon to be eclipsed by Islam, when it reaches 1.15 billion adherents. His base is morphing, with Europe careening down a steady path of secularization, socialism, moral relativism and declining populations (all clear harbingers of decline).

His high growth constituencies are nearly all from Second and Third World nations - this is where the action is for Catholicism. It is also the battleground for souls.

In Islam, Benedict sees not only an existential threat to his base, but a competitor in his target markets. Therefore, what better than to probe it, goad it, criticize it, and marginalize it in the minds of the unconverted? This process will be revealing to many who do not understand the true nature of modern Islam.

In Benedict, Islam sees the persona and office of the very thing it craves, and sadly lacks - a global, supreme leader. If Islam had such a persona, he would have thrown out the heretics and the radicals long ago. In this aspect, he is both frightening and attractive to Islamists, and they both fear and respect him tremendously. His criticisms will sting.

Benedict's papacy is probably the last that will ignore the lingering effects of millennia of hyper-male power holding by the machine bureaucracy that is Catholicism.

His successor must deal with churches without priests, anointed men counseling the married in areas they can know nothing of from experience, and the tragic legacy of the abuse of boys by homosexual priests. He is the old guard, wishes he could transform his own church, and will try to do so, but quietly.

Our bet is that he will do the greater good, and seek to transform the world's current chief source of discontent, and greatest threat.

Benedict, in his heart of hearts, also carries much guilt with him. Remember, he was a Hitler Youth. In his heart, it does not matter why he joined, what matters is what he became a part of. And so, expect his years to be marked by actions reflective of the shame and anger he bears at his past of having been a tool of Nazism. This should not be underestimated.

This is extremely important, because his worldview is one largely shaped by an understanding of the fact that sometimes, humankind develops cancer. Nazism and Radical Islam share very much in common - not the least of which is the destruction of Israel. Benedict gets this, and would be remiss if he did not bring the flock to an equally troubling and eye-opening realization.

We expect much more of such criticisms from Benedict, and perhaps his successors. We also feel that such criticisms will at best serve to unite The West, as Islam reacts, while avoiding the lingering issues bedeviling the Catholic church.

The real question in our mind is, how will thinking Catholics in Europe react to a direct philosophical confrontation with Islamists? Isn't it high time for the church to fix home first, and then look outside its glass walls, casting stones?

XLV - Religious Intolerance

Religious intolerance, wherever it exists, is wholly unacceptable. Currently, the practical effects of the actions of Radical Islam are the greatest manifestation of religious intolerance existent on today's world stage.

American Dreamers have read the core teachings of Islam, and find this religion to be largely admirable. However, several brief excerpts from the Holy Qur'an are very useful in gathering the worldview of the *average* Muslim.

This wonderful and formerly enlightened world religion, which once brought knowledge and tolerance to many in the Umma, has now been hijacked by a cancerous band of petty radicals. Just a quick reading of the world's news can well answer whether this religion, in the hands of its extremists, its desperados and its failures of the world, remains peaceful.

Know them by their works.

Sura 9.5 reads " ...then fight and slay those who join other gods with Allah wherever you find them; besiege them, siege them, lay in wait for them with every kind of ambush."

Other Suras also propagate violence against people of other religions.

[9:29] "You shall fight back against those who do not believe in GOD, nor in the Last Day, nor do they prohibit what GOD and His messenger have prohibited, nor do they abide by the religion of truth - among those who received the scripture - until they pay the due tax, willingly or unwillingly."

[9:4] "If the idol worshipers sign a peace treaty with you, and do not violate it, nor band together with others against you, you shall fulfill your treaty with them until the expiration date. GOD loves the righteous."

[9:5] "Once the Sacred Months are past, (and they refuse to make peace) you may kill the idol worshipers when you encounter them, punish them, and resist every move they make. If they repent and observe the Contact Prayers (Salat) and give the obligatory charity (Zakat), you shall let them go. GOD is Forgiver, Most Merciful. "

[9:6] "If one of the idol worshipers sought safe passage with you, you shall grant him safe passage, so that he can hear the word of GOD, then send him back to his place of security. That is because they are people who do not know."

Radical Islam, like Christian Nazism, is anything but peaceful. It is a cancer.

Bill Buckley, shortly after the vicious attacks of 9/11/01, was quoted as saying, "If this is jihad, then bring it on."

American Dreamers recognize that all of humankind is capable of the worst acts of religious intolerance, and place our bets on the values of wealth accumulation, religious tolerance and personal liberty.

XLVI - Transformational Leadership

Transformational leaders, to be effective, must maintain their credibility. Each let-down, every promise made but not delivered - the totality of repeated instances of a leader's behaving differently from what they preach, reduces their power, and their potential to transform.

Perhaps this is why we most hate leaders who tell us how to behave, and then are "caught in the act" behaving otherwise?

More commonly, what hurts our perception of our leaders most is an attitude of "Do as I say, not as I do."

We're reminded here of the parent in the 1950s, cigarette dangling from lower lip, chiding their youngster to "Never smoke!"

Or, former President Clinton, emotionally expressing his principled opposition to school vouchers, while his daughter Chelsea attended private schools.

Or, think only of the Bible thumping hypocritical preacher who got "caught in the act."

These examples are endless - and amusing, if taken cynically. The fact is, **we expect more** from our leaders. In some cultures, the leadership problem is so bad, that people sadly expect **less** from their leaders.

As you have already surmised, lying to customers is a sure recipe for disaster. Leaders who lie are especially at risk.

Think only of the very recent past:

Clinton lied about Lewinsky when he said, "Now you listen to me and you listen good, I did not have sexual relations with that woman....Ms Lewinski." From that point in his Presidency, he never again passed a significant piece of legislation.

Bush Senior lied when he said "Read My Lips - No New Taxes," and then raised them. He was soon thrown out of office after his own party revolted in the elections of '92.

The list goes on: **Nixon** and the Watergate cover-up, **Kennedy** and the quid-pro-quo removal of our Jupiter missiles from Turkey in exchange for the Russian blink in 1962...**Bush Junior** and WMD...and on it goes.

The question is, why would a leader, to be transformational, ever want to subject themselves to the mental trigonometry of having to guess whether or not her/his lies will harm anyone?

There is a **better**, *easier* way.

Think of the power of the key leader to transform with single-minded goals.

Think of the difference between the United States of America in the 7.4 seconds it took a brash young transformative leader named John Fitzgerald Kennedy to challenge, "Before this decade is out...I propose that we send a man to the moon, and bring him back safely..."

One man, *one* vision, *one* promise, *one* nation, *one* world, *an entire species* immediately and irreversibly transformed from the earth bound, to the space far-ing.

Dreamers bet that The Creator smiled in those 7.4 seconds. We still do today each time we think of the moment.

Americans - we can think of many more. We want your ideas. We want your dreams.

XLVII - Diversity and the Civil Rights Act of 1964

American Dreamers are gratified to see many employers going beyond the amount of melanin in one's skin in the careful process of examining and respecting diversity.

By 2049, "white" people will comprise 49.9% of the total population, rendering the Civil Rights Act of 1964 moot. The Supreme Court planned for this long ago - deciding that this Act was a necessary, *but temporary* solution to the problem of equal rights and access for protected groups.

We anticipate smiling in our rocking chairs on that golden morning when "white" become a "minority"!

XLVIII - Zen Coaching & Leadership

For a brief respite, let us more closely examine the meaning of the Japanese word *Zen*, which is borrowed from the mother language, Chinese, (Asia's Latin - Chinese is the root of Japanese, Korean and Vietnamese) in which the character is pronounced *Ren.*

The character literally means, **to recognize the self**. Practitioners of the **Zen** religion place a very high value on not living in the past, or in the future, but in the very moment one finds oneself within. Everything except what is happening in the moment we are living in is a distraction, clouding our reality, like dust on a mirror.

Remember Master Yoda training young Luke in Star Wars? Very **zen**.

When practiced, this philosophy can be emancipating, sharply increases one's focus, which is an especially valuable leadership trait in today's hyper noisy work world.

Sports fans need think only of the amazing three Dynasties of *Bulls* and *Lakers* coach **Phil Jackson**, owner of 10 NBA rings, one as a player with the New York Knicks, where Jackson was known as 'elbows', and first emerged as a leader.

In the late 1980s *Chicago Bulls*, Jackson inherited a team that **Doug Collins** had taken to the opening rounds of the playoffs, and that had never won a championship, in spite of having **Michael Jordan** and **Scottie Pippen**.

Jackson immediately went to work, teaching his players to focus purely on their own roles on the team, mastering these first. Jackson also taught his players to seek and master 'mind zone', a state of awareness that drowns out all distractions between one's fingertips and the very center of the rim of the basket, including nagging opposing players, and deafening crowd noise.

Six NBA championships in the next eight years later, player after player commented on the fact that it was this role playing and mind zone that enabled them to become great, with legendary performances. **Steve Kerr** became the best three point shooter in the NBA. **Tony Kukoc** became the best sixth man in the NBA. **M.J.** became the best point guard in the NBA. **Scottie Pippen** became the best defenseman in the NBA. After developing these role players, Jackson masterfully rotated his three centers, (Longley, Wennington and Cartwright) forging an unstoppable three-headed monster that could inflict 15 fouls per game, unselfishly feeding the Tex Winters *Triangle Offense.*

Doubters said it wasn't Jackson's leadership that created the Bulls dynasty; doubters said it wasn't his practice of **zen**.

Jackson then went to Los Angeles, and built a continually under-achieving *Lakers* team into a 3 time NBA Champion, using the same **zen** principles, built upon a lonely, erratic center named **Shaquille O'Neill**, and a brash, selfish guard named **Kobe Bryant**. Amazingly, Jackson repeated the successful formula!

Keep in mind Red Auerbach never came close to doing this in his 10 Championships with one team (*Celtics*).

Today, managers and leaders actively seek to study this stuff called **zen**, because it works. Create role players on the team. Get the players to focus on the moment. Ask the players to act unselfishly.

Vince Lombardi, winner of the first two SuperBowls and five NFL Championships, in his short time as head coach of the **Green Bay Packers** between 1959 and 1968, once said:

"Success rests not upon ability, but upon commitment, pride, motivation, and above all else, the denial of self for the good of the team. This is the new leadership."

Dreamers know that Phil Jackson gets this. The question for us, fellow Americans, is this: Will we model some **zen** for our country?

XLIX - Stem Cell Research

Dreamers are convinced of the high value and tremendous potential of stem cell research, and concur with the majority of Americans that this avenue of research merits rapid development, to include government funding.

American researchers are currently being left in the dust by our East Asian friends, thanks in no small measure to our President, who favors limiting stem cell lines.

This policy is akin to telling your best students to "Go research, but don't use more than one room of the library."

We are also convinced that the use of embryonic stem cells, taken from embryos that would otherwise be destroyed, is an ethical practice. There are over 400,000 such little people in storage here in the United States, frozen and isolated as we speak. What a waste of God's tools (and insult to the Creator) to so handle, and potentially trash, human beings.

We are also convinced that, eventually, the use of live stem cells from living human donors will render moot the current controversies.

L - Malnourishment and Hunger in America

In our modern day and age, no greater inexcusable American scourge exists than that of malnourishment and hunger.

Dreamers are united behind powerful efforts to limit the extent of hunger, and salute organizations like the Boy Scouts of America for their noble efforts to eradicate this lingering plague, through the Scouting For Food movement.

Through a nationwide adoption of the wise methodology used by the Scouts, led by the Food and Drug Administration, the American Dream Party advocates for the set aside of a week-long nationwide food drive, to be annually held during the week before the Thanksgiving Holiday, with volunteers from throughout the United States collecting donations of non-perishable items and canned food.

The National Food Drive will commence with food donation bags being distributed to volunteers; day two will see bag distribution maps carefully plotted and posted; day three will see volunteers going door to door hanging food collection bags, with drop-off points at grocery stores, fire stations and willing businesses; the fourth day will see food bags collected and transported to food distribution centers; day five will see the food sorted and packaged for transshipment to food banks; the sixth day will see the shipping of collected items to food banks; with day seven of the drive completing the national effort with materials disposal and clean-up.

Dreamers anticipate the National Food Drive joining the great traditions of the Thanksgiving Holiday, as American as turkey dinner, football, and giving thanks to the Creator for this nation's bounty.

LI - On Personal Ethics

In the course of our years in life, with family, in our travels, in the workplace, in our houses of worship, taking Dreamers around the world, thrusting them into many varied and interesting experiences, we have enjoyed the pleasure of discovering many, indisputable "ethical gold nuggets." These pearls of wisdom reflect profoundly upon our core ethical beliefs, and for the purposes of this book, the author will provide them, attributing authorship, and adding brief reflective comments.

"[W]hen the shoe fits, the foot is forgotten; when the belt fits, the belly is forgotten; when the heart is right, "for" and "against" are forgotten."

-Chuang Tzu (c. 369-c. 286 B.C.), Theologian and writer

There is no better state of mind than that of being in the right, out for nothing less than the maximum good, with an enlightened self-interest as one's guiding spirit.

"Brevity explained isn't."

-T.T. Wimplefurt

The older we get, the harder it is to suffer fools, and the more precious becomes the passage of time. One comes to appreciate those who respect the time of others, and models one's behaviors as such.

"Education's purpose is to replace an empty mind with an open one."

-Chinese Proverb

Dreamers believe in this purpose of education, but also try their best to imbue this sense in fellow citizens.

"Shoot for the moon. Even if you miss, you'll land among the stars."

-Les Brown

In working with many seekers over the years, Dreamers have discovered that there is precious little fault to find in the intentions of those who over reach.

"If you aren't fired with enthusiasm, you'll be fired with enthusiasm."

-Vince Lombardi

Dreamers have found that, although in business one should certainly follow the money, in human services, one should follow the ideas, looking for those who have a passion and an enthusiasm for what they propose.

"Be who you are and say what you feel, because those who mind don't matter and those who matter don't mind."

-Dr. Suess

It all goes back to the clever lyrics to the Beatles' song, *"Nowhere Man,"* and Dreamers do their best not to fall into the comfortable trap of making safe plans for nobody, out of the desire to offend no one.

"If opportunity doesn't knock, build a door."

-Milton Berle

What a cool way of reminding us to get out and create our own success, and that this process is owned by us, in our hands.

"Don't waste time learning the tricks of the trade. Instead, learn the trade."

-H. Jackson Brown, Jr.

Dreamers have learned that no matter what course of business we find ourselves working in, an honest treatment of the truth behind the product will go much farther than gimmickry. Someone once said it best, advising us to remember that, in our good works, we are not just selling used cars – it is all about transforming peoples' lives.

"The trouble with learning from experience is that you never graduate."

-Doug Larson

Great wisdom and satisfaction comes from knowing what you don't know, and relishing the opportunity of a never ending learning experience.

"If you think education is expensive, try ignorance!"

-Andy Rooney

More lives are ruined by well intentioned people who make decisions based upon anything other than the facts.

"Your majesty, enlightenment is not a matter of age. A tiny spark of fire has the power to burn down a whole city. A small poisonous snake can kill you in an instant. A baby prince has the potential of a king. And a young monk has the capacity of becoming enlightened and changing the world."

-Excerpt from a conversation about The Buddha

As youthful members of an aging culture, it is a source of tremendous frustration when trying to get one's views across to people who look down upon youthful inexperience. American Dreamers have come to find that youth brings with it an almost magical perspective that seeks not, why a thing won't work, but rather, why it can.

"Done is beautiful."

-Robin Schultz

In spite of our procrastinations and endless hesitancies, keeping one's eyes on the prize, envisioning the feeling of getting the task done, is a sound motivator.

"The most important thing I have learned over the years is the difference between taking one's work seriously and taking one's self seriously. The first is imperative, and the second disastrous."

—Margaret Fontey

This piece of ethical wisdom reminds us to seek projects that are worth the time, and the outcomes of which are worth defending.

"One ought never to turn one's back on a threatened danger and try to run away from it. If you do that, you will double the danger. But if you meet it promptly and without flinching, you will reduce the danger by half."

-Sir Winston Churchill

American Dreamers well remember that for more than a decade, Churchill obsessed upon the rising threat of Nazism in Central Europe, helping to prepare a sleeping citizenry for a growing cancerous threat. Today, one is reminded of this spirit when considering the rising threat of the cancer we call Radical Islam.

"Do your duty in all things. You cannot do more. You should never wish to do less."

-Robert E. Lee

There is no better feeling than to look back upon the times in one's life when maximum efforts were being expended on a good cause. Such is the rallying cry of this book's call to action.

"A vote is like a rifle: its usefulness depends on the character of the user."

-President Theodore Roosevelt

Americans need only to hark back to the 5-to-4 decision by the Supreme Court of the United States of America to keep homosexuals out of the leadership of the Boy Scouts of America back in 2000. Just one decisive vote by Chief Justice Rehnquist set back, by decades, the radical homosexual lobby's agenda, saving a worthy youth movement from certain destruction.

"Persistence is the face of tenacity."

-Dr. Tim Dosemagen

If one proposes a good idea, and it is not accepted, one should propose that idea again, and again, and again, until it is accepted. There is no shame in persistence in the pursuit of a greater good.

"Do not imagine that personal relationships will run themselves. Like jobs, they are valuable in proportion to the amount of effort they demand."

-W. H. Auden (1907- 1973), Poet

American Dreamers have come to value the time it takes to stay in touch with those we hold dear. People, like all else that lives, need our care and feeding.

"Instead of loving your enemies, treat your friends a little better."

-Edgar Watson Howe (1853-1937), Journalist

There is so much more to value in taking care of one's friends and allies than in navel gazing at why one's enemies choose to hate. Enemies do not deserve one's time nearly so much as do friends.

"We must not believe the many who say that only free people ought to be educated, but we should rather believe the philosophers who say that only the educated are free."

-Epictetus

Dreamers disavow the intellectual snobbery some espouse in their selective distribution of the application of a sound education. None are more reprehensible than those who refuse to allow educational vouchers for parents who desire to send their children to private primary or secondary education.

"Eat and drink with your relatives; do business with strangers."

-Greek Proverb

Dreamers agree that this ethical principle not only results in a slimmer waistline, but also more total business conducted.

"The brain is like a muscle. When we think well, we feel good."

-Carl Sagan (1934-1996), Scientist

American Dreamers are most ill at ease when in realizing that they have not taken the time to learn the subject, or the issue at hand. The worst of all conditions is when this state of mind is combined with fatigue.

"Horse sense is what keeps horses from betting on what people will do."

-Mark Twain

Would that people could use more horse sense in their daily lives!

"Anger of the mind is poison to the soul."

-Ecuadorian Proverb

Dreamers feel physically worse off when angry, per-haps borne out of a rise in blood pressure from the negative emotions and fear attached to anger. To extend this feeling to the mind, which is, after all, physically connected to the body, one can only imagine what damage anger wreaks there, and beyond.

"Anger is one of the sinners of the soul."

-Thomas Fuller

A quick study of history finds that on many occasions, poor (or even evil) decisions were made in a state of anger. The responsibility for these decisions must stay with the person who makes them, and are therefore potentially corrupting.

"Business? It's quite simple. It's other people's money."

-Alexandre Dumas the Younger

How often one finds oneself making business decisions as if the money one is throwing around is someone else's. Instead of acting in this way, Dreamers strive to conduct business as if his their own personal interests were hanging on the success or failure of the venture at hand.

"Get a little better every day."

-Roman Proverb

Would that even on our worst days, we would keep in mind the fact that all of our experiences are making us better, as long as we have the proper intentions in mind, and keep our eyes and ears open.

"Success rests not upon ability, but upon commitment, pride, motivation, and above all else, the denial of self for the good of the team. This is the new leadership."

-Vincent Lombardi

This philosophy gives hope to American Dreamers, and answers the question of how a young man who was cut from his high school basketball team could go on to become Michael Jordan. When tired and frustrated, we will do well to call upon the reserves which exist in the knowledge that our effort is contributing to The Team, no matter how small or great its membership.

"Ex nihilo nihil fit." {Without something there exists nothing.}

-Marcus Aurelius

Dreamers believe that it is far better to attempt something, even if doing it has risks attached, and the effort requires ongoing refinement, than it is to let a need remain unfulfilled, under cover of endless feasibility studies, or consensus building discussion. There is more to be feared in inaction than in action.

"NFL…Not For Long! Put your education first. You need something to fall back on after athletics."

-Emery Moorehead, Tight End, SuperBowl XX Winning Chicago Bears

This former Chicago Bear, perhaps as a result of too many concussions while playing a violent sport, developed myasthenia gravis, a chronic, debilitative disease that eats away at one's physical skills. Mr. Moorehead's admonishment, often shared with youngsters, is a lesson well worth remembering.

"Your perfect day is within you, every day."

-Heather Cornell

Attitude, as Charles Swindoll has said, is what we choose to make of our days. American Dreamers, when working through the few early waking moments of a bad day, frequently falls back on this philosophy, which sure beats going out and hating the whole world.

"No good thing is pleasant to possess without good friends to share it with."

-Lucius Aennius Seneca

What becomes most apparent to us as we age is the fact that friends are very important in this life, and good friends are exceedingly rare.

"Faith is the daring of the soul to go farther than it can see."

-Unknown

Dreamers love this quote, and find its innate truth to be profound.

"Progress is impossible without change; and those who cannot change their minds cannot change anything."

-George Bernard Shaw

This quote is particularly useful in teaching change management, and Dreamers are careful to describe the thoughtful, painstaking process required to actually change one's mind. It begins with challenging assumptions, then overcoming conventions, and finally, bravely putting aside comfortable consistencies. This is hard work, and heavy intellectual lifting, and not what people go out and look for.

"The worst pessimist is the lazy optimist."

-T.T. Wimplefurt

American Dreamers well remember working under political "leaders" whom, while doing very little to improve the tactical situation, would always state that the strategic situation was improving, and that we were 'turning the corner.' The dissonance between actions and words never sit well, and it proved to us that people who are positive can be quite lazy.

"We cannot direct the wind, but we can adjust the sails."

-Unknown

This statement sums up so well the ownership each of us has for what we do each day to improve our lives, and the worlds we dwell within.

"In the middle of difficulty lies opportunity."

-Albert Einstein

Dreamers try to keep this philosophy in mind when having a 'hard day.'

"Take each of the heads of warring nations, give each a 50 pound sack of horse manure, lock them in a room, and let them fight it out."

-John Cage

Would that one could solve the international crises *du jour* by locking our leaders in a room and letting them fight it out. Though overly simplistic, the thought amuses, could potentially save lives, and is not outside the realm of possibility.

"Let us remember, at this dawn of a new century, that history is not over. We dwell in a continually incomplete history. The lesson of our unfinished humanity is that when we exclude we are made poorer, and when we include we are made richer. None of us will ever be able to find the humanity within us unless we are able to find it first in others."

-Carlos Fuentes

The more we travel, the more people we meet, the harder it becomes to remain prejudiced against any group of people. It is by getting out of our comfortable crib that we begin to discover our world, and the reality of life is that this analogy works for each and every opportunity a person has to grow.

"What we do in life, echoes in eternity."

-Maximus Decimus Maridius (from the 2000 motion picture, *Gladiator*, masterfully directed by the great *Ridley Scott)*

What we do counts. Our actions are everlasting. We may leave behind only genes and ideas on this earth, but our actions in this lifetime change the world.

"Reason is and ought to be the slave of the passion. Reason can tell us what to do; only the passions can will us to do it."

-David Hume

This quote reminds Dreamers that it is OK to go beyond cool logic, because it is passionate people who are the most fun to work with.

"What's the difference between a taxidermist and a tax collector? The taxidermist takes only your skin."

-Mark Twain

American Dreamers despise tax collectors, and wishes the entire business of taxation could be streamlined by adoption of a flat sales tax on all goods, period.

"Rumors = My interpretation of what you haven't told me."

-Ronald Noble

How often one is tempted to dream up information, when the easiest thing to do is to ask the source.

"The task ahead of us is never as great as the power behind us."

-Ralph Waldo Emerson

All work shrinks when we remember that, if the work is good, the power of creation is behind it. This is the flow of nature, one of life's greatest unwritten laws, and why those who destroy are always destroyed.

"To love what you do, and feel that it matters; how could anything be more fun?"

-Katherine Graham

Dreamers have found that it's not just enough to make good money, but to do so while engaged in a sound cause, with tangible fruits. Would that this ethic could have been in place when the writer began his working journey!

"The world will little note nor long remember what we say here, but it can never forget what they did here. It is for us the living rather to be dedicated here to the unfinished work which they who fought here have thus far so nobly advanced. It is rather for us to be here dedicated to the great task remaining before us—that from these honored dead we take increased devotion to that cause for which they gave the last full measure of devotion—that we here highly resolve that these dead shall not have died in vain, that this nation under God shall have a new birth of freedom, and that government of the people, by the people, for the people shall not perish from the earth."

-President Abraham Lincoln, The Gettysburg Address, 1863

People who die in the name of a noble cause never die in vain. What beautiful, simply eloquent words.

"Door goes up, door goes down."

-Homer J. Simpson

This quote comes from a simpleton who is lampooned as such on TV. Yet, we are moved by the fact that all of us were simple once, thinking as children, perceiving things in an uncomplicated, clearly defined world. One wonders if there is any benefit to be gained from the avoidance of over-intellectualization.

Dr. Tim Dosemagen

About The Author

DR. TIMOTHY B. DOSEMAGEN

Born and reared in Kenosha Wisconsin, Dr. Tim Dosemagen resides with his family in Southern Arizona.

Dr. Dosemagen served in the United States Air Force for 7 years during the Carter and Reagan Administrations as a Cryptologic Analyst, reporting to the National Security Agency. During his 3 years of gathering intelligence in the Republic of Korea, China launched its first submarine launched ballistic missile, while suffering several significant pilot and aircraft defections.

Dosemagen was decorated with the Air Force Achievement Medal (1985), the Air Force Commendation Medal (1986), and received the Joint Service Achievement Medal for "...preparing for publication a substantive report of immense benefit within the intelligence community..." conferred in the city of Washington, by Lt. Gen William Odom, DIRNSA, on April 6th, 1987.

After completing full-time government service in 1987, Dosemagen briefly instructed Chinese Mandarin in the Kenosha Unified School District, before joining the professional service of the Boy Scouts of America where he worked for 11 years, finishing as Director of Field Service with the Northeast Illinois

Council, based in Highland Park, Illinois. His service area extended from the northern suburbs of Chicago to southeastern Wisconsin, and he served over 18,000 youngsters and 4,000 adult volunteers in 375 local Scout groups.

Dosemagen briefly served as La Leche League International's Director of Operations, and then as Director of Marketing and Funding for the IEF Education Foundation, a California-based organization dedicated to bridging the gap between U.S. educational opportunities and students from China, Taiwan, Korea and East Asia. IEF has offices in Taipei, Taiwan, Washington, D.C. and Shanghai, China.

He then served as a consultant to Central Michigan University's innovative College of Distance and Distributed Learning, and then continued his consultancy with the Bright China Management Institute in Beijing.

He served as Executive Director, ABC Child Development, Inc., a $14,000,000 human service agency with a staff of 256 located in El Monte, California.

Presently, Dosemagen serves as Director of Academic Affairs with the University of Phoenix's Southern Arizona Campus, and instructs 29 courses in the Graduate School of Business and Management, the Undergraduate School of Business and Management, the Colleges of Health and Human Services, Arts & Sciences, and Education, instructing coursework in management, leadership, organizational behavior, international education, critical thinking, employment law and effective written communications.

In addition to his B.A. in Asian Studies (University of Maryland, 1987), Dosemagen holds a Masters in Human Services (Murray State University, 1996), and received his Doctorate in Education – Management of Programs (Nova Southeastern University, 2000).

A Paul Harris Fellow and long time Rotarian, Dosemagen is also a Vigil Honor Member of the Order of the Arrow, an Eagle Scout, an American Legionnaire, was honored by the American Inn of Court of Northern Illinois with its 2000 Distinguished Service Award, serves on the Board of Directors of the Catalina Council, Boy Scouts of America, Tucson, Arizona, and on the Board of Directors of the Arizona Youth Partnership, a youth serving organization with statewide programs and initiatives.

In the spring of 2002, Dosemagen lectured to Chinese educational community consumers in Shanghai and Nanjing, on recent policy changes in United States immigration procedures and post-secondary educational administration, as a result of the terrorist attacks of September 11th, 2001. In the fall of 2004, he lectured in Beijing on leadership and organizational culture, while introducing the teachings of Dr. Peter F. Drucker to Chinese educational consumers.

He enjoys writing, translating, traveling, and the great outdoors. His first novel, *Prodigies* (1stBooks, 2003) was quickly followed by a collection of short stories and essays, *The Impossible* (Authorhouse, 2004), and a spy thriller set in East Asia, *The Trigger*, (Author-house, 2006).

Official Certificate of Membership in

The American Dream Party

of the United States of America

As a member of the American Dream party of the United States of America, I agree with the critical need for the continuous improvement of the American Democracy.

As an American Dreamer, I pledge on my honor to do my best to help build a better nation, under God, indivisible, with liberty and justice for all.

As an American Dreamer, I will boldly share my ideas and those of my Party with fellow Americans and citizens of the world. When challenged by those whose political ideologies disagree with mine, or those of the Party, I pledge my honor to engage on the issues with honesty, candor, openness, tolerance, compassion, respect and integrity. This particularly applies to our misguided fellow Americans who support the drunken Democratic, Republican, Libertarian, Communist, Socialist and Independent agendas.

As an American Dreamer, I pledge on my honor to do my best to unite Americans of all generations, economic strata, races, creeds, colors, orientations, religions, ideologies and political persuasions, in the common pursuit of an improved Democracy.

As an American Dreamer, I pledge on my honor to seek out, identify, and freely share skills, techniques, and opportunities for improving the lives of my fellow citizens.

As an American Dreamer, I pledge on my honor to embrace change as a continuous process of replacing fear, ignorance, superstition and intolerance with hope, expertise, the truth, and humanitarianism.

As an American Dreamer, I pledge, on my honor to remain physically fit, mentally engaged, spiritually connected, morally straight, and politically engaged.

Welcome aboard, Dreamer! Let's roll up our sleeves and get to work.

Dr. Timothy E. Dossemagen
Founder and Chairman
American Dream Party of the United States of America

Printed in the United States
69513LVS00001B/169-186